People, Politics and Economic Life

Exploring Appalachia with Quantitative Methods

Updated Second Edition

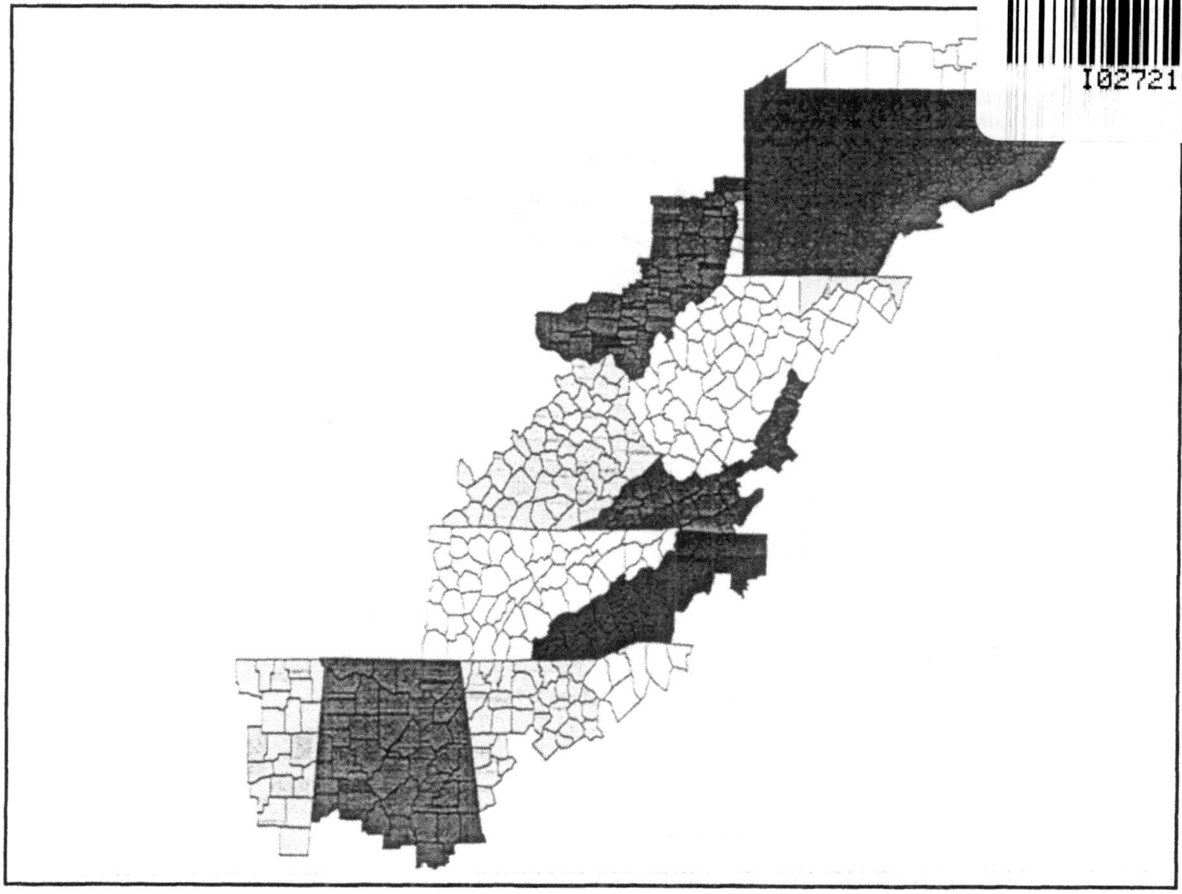

Thomas Plaut

With an overview of the Appalachian Region by Susan Emley Keefe

KENDALL/HUNT PUBLISHING COMPANY
in cooperation with
APPALACHIAN CONSORTIUM PRESS

Software created by **MicroCase** *Corporation*

3½ inch IBM-compatible diskette enclosed

The Appalachian Consortium was a non-profit educational organization composed of institutions and agencies located in Southern Appalachia. From 1973 to 2004, its members published pioneering works in Appalachian studies documenting the history and cultural heritage of the region. The Appalachian Consortium Press was the first publisher devoted solely to the region and many of the works it published remain seminal in the field to this day.

With funding from the Andrew W. Mellon Foundation and the National Endowment for the Humanities through the Humanities Open Book Program, Appalachian State University has published new paperback and open access digital editions of works from the Appalachian Consortium Press.

www.collections.library.appstate.edu/appconsortiumbooks

This work is licensed under a Creative Commons BY-NC-ND license. To view a copy of the license, visit http://creativecommons.org/licenses.

Original copyright © 1996 by the Appalachian Consortium Press.

ISBN (pbk.: alk. Paper): 978-1-4696-4134-8
ISBN (ebook): 978-1-4696-4135-5

Distributed by the University of North Carolina Press
www.uncpress.org

CONTENTS

I.	Susan Emley Keefe: Appalachia and Its People	3
II.	Exploring a Region through Quantitative Data Frequencies and Percentages	25
III.	Cultural Diversity in Appalachia Mapping, Rank Ordering and Correlation Coefficients	34
IV.	Demographics: Urbanization and Migration in Appalachia Mapping and Regression	45
V.	The Appalachian Economy I: Comparing Subregions Analysis of Variance (ANOVA) in Group Scores	57
VI.	The Economy II: Industry and Opportunity Correlations and Regressions	75
VII.	Voting Patterns and Economic Conditions Tables, χ^2, and Nonparametric Measures of Association	85
VIII.	Race and Region: Minorities in Appalachia Multiple Regression	101
IX.	A Region with Many Definitions	114
X.	The Internet: Finding New Data in The Information Age	125
Glossary		133
Codebook for the APCOUNTY File Variables		139
Suggested Readings and Media Resources by Chapter		145

Preface to the Second Edition

This edition updates the data set and responds to the insights of users over the past three years. Students, both undergraduate and graduate, report finding the book to be a good means of learning or relearning and reviewing statistical methods and consequently I've attempted to refine the commentary on data analysis. Faculty report that students can work through the material with minimal guidance and thus are prepared to talk about results--and the questions raised by the results--in class. New exercises have been added for summarizing research results, which make use of software not available at the time of the first printing (such as Microsoft's PowerPoint or Corel's Presentations).

There is a new chapter on the Appalachia as a region, which serves to balance and explicate the quantitative material and exercises. The chapter was written by Susan Emley Keefe, chair of the Department of Anthropology at Appalachian State University, who has numerous publications on the region to her credit, including Appalachian Mental Health (University Press of Kentucky, 1988).

Definitions of Appalachia have been continually changing over the past century. In his chapter on "Concept and Method" in Glen E. Lich's Regional Studies: The Interplay of Land and People (College Station, Texas, Texas A&M University Press, 1992), Terry G. Jordan describes three concepts of region: 1) the *formal*, having a homogeneity of traits; 2) the *vernacular*, which has a "broadly perceived regional self-consciousness," and 3) the *functional*. The functional region "is an area that has been organized to function politically, socially or economically" (page 20). Sue Keefe's chapter provides the evidence for Appalachia as a formal region, which some might also argue contains evidence for a vernacular one. Appalachia, as defined by the Appalachian Regional Commission, is best described as a functional region.

There is a new chapter on the Internet to walk students through obtaining information at the national, regional and county levels. The Internet chapter provides links to public and private agencies, educational institutions and citizens' groups involved in the Appalachian region. A data file adapted from this chapter is included on the disk accompanying the book. Users can sign onto the Internet, then pull up either the WordPerfect or Microsoft Word "Internet launcher" file and click on the blue hyperlinks to access web sites described in the text.

The rapid changes of the Information Age created some challenges for this edition. There was new data to be incorporated since the first publication three years ago. Six new variables on population, income and poverty have been added to the data set. The mapping software could not be changed and consequently seven counties added by Appalachian Regional Commission to its definition of the region in 1998 are missing: Macon and Hale counties in Alabama; Elbert, Hart and Yalobusha in Georgia, and Montgomery and Rockbridge in Virginia. The chapter on the Internet was designed in part to overcome this problem; users can access the Commission's web site for data on these and other counties.

A note on software: Since this student version of the MicroCase software is DOS based, *Windows users can move out of the program into other applications by holding down the Alt key and pressing the Tab key.* The program can be entered again with a mouse click on the bar at the bottom of the monitor screen. The APCOUNTY data file can be accessed by the complete MicroCase Analysis System statistical package available in many colleges and universities. This package provides a full range of statistical procedures and the ability to convert the file for use by other statistical programs such as SPSS.

October 2001

Preface

Appalachia often has been portrayed as a distant mountain region inhabited by less-than-reputable holdovers from the American frontier who somehow escaped the blessings of modernization. This stereotype sadly misses the mark. Extending from New York to Mississippi, Appalachia is as varied as any region in the United States, containing great differences in geography, climate and culture. Like many places in America, it includes areas facing economic hardship as well as areas enjoying growth in industry, population and per capita income. It has both wealth and poverty, isolated rural hamlets and metropolitan areas. Each year, thousands of people hike its mountain trails, raft its whitewater streams and pack into its music and storytelling festivals.

As a region of contrasts, Appalachia can be viewed as a "slice of the American pie." Yet its geography and resources have also made it unique. The coal industry has dominated the central part of the region with widespread impacts. A long tradition of mountain family farming, especially in Southern Appalachia, has emphasized the importance of self sufficiency, social equality and the bonds of kinship and community. The region has been the target of a number of experiments in social change and engineering, from turn-of-the-century missionaries to the poverty warriors, dollars and politics turned loose in the Appalachian Regional Development Act of 1960s. Size is significant: Appalachia includes 399 counties (12.7 percent of all U.S. counties) in 13 states (26 percent of all the states). It is big enough to reflect the complexities of late 20th century America and yet small enough to retain its own history and cultural identity. It provides a wealth of data for people interested in regional history, economics, modernization and social change.

This workbook is designed to provide the means for exploring issues facing any American region, as well as Appalachia. It can be used as a supporting text in courses on regional studies, geography, history and the social sciences, or simply as a source for people thinking about their own communities. Readers will work with data from the U.S. Bureau of the Census, Bureau of Economic Analysis, Appalachian Regional Commission and other agencies. A computer disk containing the necessary software is included so that, as the book raises questions, the reader can find answers on any IBM-compatible computer with 640K of memory (RAM) and a VGA graphics card. The disk contains a data file with 96 variables for the 399 Appalachian counties, along with a trimmed-down version of the MicroCase statistics package.

May 1996

Acknowledgments

A number of people have assisted in the development of this volume. Ron Eller and Gordon McKinney, who direct Appalachian Centers at the University of Kentucky and Berea College, respectively, reviewed the text from the perspective of their years of research and work in the mountains. Marian Plaut brought her talents as an editor, therapist and spouse to the manuscript, as did June Trevor, a colleague at Western North Carolina Community Health Research Services at the Mountain Area Health Education Center in Asheville. Mars Hill College President Fred Bentley offered funding for research and publication of the workbook. John Payne, the college's Dean for Learning Resources, funded the development of the book's computer map and the research that linked the county-by-county data to it. The students who beta-tested the exercises were Jamie Willis, Robert Gouge, Joy Greene, Josh Sparks, Sherry Wagner, Condalisa Hankton, Marne Crisp, Hope Lloyd, Alicia Payne and Kara Hensley. Phil Obermiller, Dick Couto, Ray Rapp, Walter Stroud and Ken Sanchagrin provided counsel and support at various stages in the development of this project. Judy Slater, Laurie Pederson and George Peery reviewed the manuscript for the second edition.

William Fox reviewed the manuscript with humor and a sharp eye for statistics. His text, *Social Statistics using MicroCase,* was a primary tool in my developing the manuscript; its glossary served as a template for my own. The Appalachian Regional Commission's Salim Kablawi, Judith Maher and Ann Anderson were helpful in accessing the latest available data for Appalachia's 399 counties. MicroCase Corporation's David Smetters arranged for the production of the computerized map which is so central to the book and patiently gave advice and counsel in the use of his company's statistical analysis package.

The Author

Thomas Plaut is a Professor of Sociology and Director of the Center for Assessment and Research Alliances (CARA) at Mars Hill College, a small liberal arts college founded by farmers for their children in the mountains of Western North Carolina near Asheville in the mid nineteenth century. He is a consultant and trainer for hospitals, hospices and health systems and has authored articles on research methods, regional issues and cultural differences between service providers and rural clients and staff. He received his A.B. degree from Harvard, M.A. from American University and Ph.D. from the Union Graduate School.

For Marian

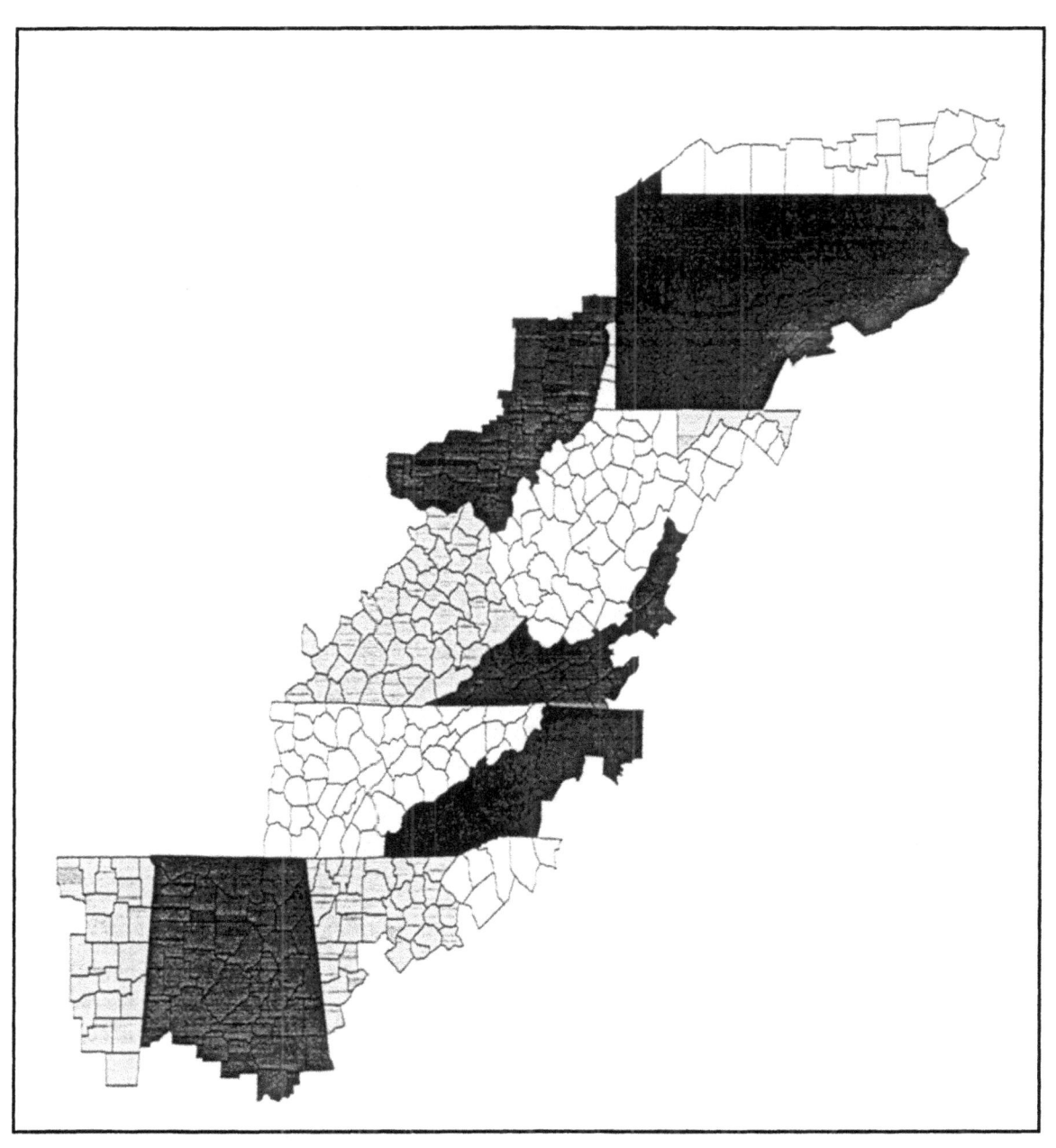

**Appalachia as defined by the
Appalachian Regional Commission in 1996:
399 counties in 13 states**

I. Appalachia and Its People

Susan Emley Keefe
Appalachian State University

Defining the Region

The name "Appalachia" originates in the geography of the region. The most distinctive regional feature is the Appalachian Mountain chain, which was named by early Spanish explorers who borrowed the term from an Indian tribe, the Appalachee, in northern Florida (Raitz and Ulack 1991). Appalachia consists of four physiographic regions: the eastern piedmont, the Blue Ridge Mountains, the Greater Appalachian Valley, and the Allegheny-Cumberland Plateau. The Blue Ridge range was created almost 500 million years ago when land masses from east and west moved together and the stress caused the earth to buckle into parallel ridges. The Alleghenies are newer. There was a shallow sea where the Greater Appalachian Valley is now. The sea receded and the earth beneath buckled, creating the upland plateau area. The north-south Appalachian mountain chain, stretching from Alabama to New York, makes east-west travel difficult, heightening the importance of the Greater Appalachian Valley as a transportation route through the region.

As a geographic and cultural area within a nation, there are no fixed boundaries defining Appalachia. Geographers tend to be inclusive, extending the regional boundaries to the edges of the piedmont and plateau provinces. They often vary, nevertheless, in marking the exact regional boundaries, taking into consideration differences in elevation, climate, soil type, and cultural environment (Raitz and Ulack 1991).

On the other hand, sociocultural studies tend to put greater emphasis on cultural features, emphasizing a core area in the southern highlands. In his classic study, The Southern Highlander and His Homeland (1921), John C. Campbell included West Virginia and portions of 8 other states: Alabama, Georgia, South Carolina, North Carolina, Tennessee, Kentucky, Virginia, and Maryland. He called the region bounded by natural topography "a land of mountains, valleys, and plateaus." He also noted its physical isolation, culturally homogeneous heritage, and stable population.

In a notable economic-based survey of the region in 1962, The Southern Appalachian Region: A Survey, Thomas Ford reduced Campbell's region to the heartland, including West Virginia and portions of 6 other states: Alabama, Georgia, North Carolina, Tennessee, Kentucky, and Virginia. While Campbell emphasized culture and geography in defining the region, Ford focused on the lack of economic development as a defining characteristic.

In 1965, the federal government established the Appalachian Regional Commission (ARC) and defined the Appalachian region by the criterion of economic need. West Virginia and portions of 12 other states (Mississippi, Alabama, Georgia, South Carolina, North Carolina, Tennessee, Kentucky, Virginia, Maryland, Ohio, Pennsylvania, and New York) are eligible for monies from the multi-billion dollar economic development program established by the Appalachian Regional Development Act.

Political maneuvering by governors hoping to include underdeveloped portions of their states added areas never before considered part of the Appalachian region. The primary considerations for inclusion were, finally, geographic contiguity and economic underdevelopment marked by lack of jobs and forced migration, overspecialization of the economy, a high rate of poverty, low rates of education, and poor health facilities. The purpose of the ARC is to rectify these conditions with highway construction, health services, educational and sanitation facilities, and small business expansion. As defined by the ARC, Appalachia has 26.5 million people, which is 11.7% of the US population (US Bureau of the Census 1980).

> This chapter has been adapted from "Appalachian Americans: The Formation of Reluctant Ethnics" in Gregory R. Campbell, ed., Many Americas: Critical Perspectives on Race, Racism and Ethnicity. Dubuque, IO: Kendall/Hunt 1998.

Recognizing the diversity encompassed within the borders of its definition of Appalachia, the ARC identifies three subregions: Northern, Central, and Southern Appalachia (ARC 1965). Northern Appalachia, the largest of the three, includes designated counties in New York, Pennsylvania, Ohio, Maryland, and northern West Virginia. It is also the most populous and the most urban, taking in seven US Census-designated Standard Metropolitan Statistical Areas (SMSAs) including Erie, PA, and Binghamton, NY. Northern Appalachia is an old industrialized area based on nineteenth century coal, steel, and railroad development which declined in prominence following the Depression and the growth of highway transportation in other parts of the country. The older factories became obsolete, cities began to deteriorate physically, and many people migrated out.

Central Appalachia is composed of counties in eastern Kentucky, northwestern Tennessee, southern West Virginia, and southwestern Virginia. This subregion encompasses the smallest area and has the smallest population. It is also the most rural subregion, and includes no US Census SMSAs. It has the poorest population because it is dominated by a single-resource economy: coal. There are rich deposits of bituminous coal, and Central Appalachia holds the main US deposit of anthracite coal. The region's economy fluctuates with the coal economy resulting in boom-and-bust cycles which, along with increasing mechanization in the mines, have created huge waves of out-migration, especially in the mid-twentieth century.

Southern Appalachia takes in counties in eastern Tennessee, southwestern Virginia, North Carolina, South Carolina, Georgia, Alabama and Mississippi. It is the most rapidly growing subregion due to an expanding economy based on industry, recreation, and tourism. Historically an agricultural and timber region, industrialization came relatively late to Southern Appalachia in the last half of the twentieth century. Growing urbanization and its associated social problems have affected the subregion, which contains six US Census SMSAs, including Knoxville, TN, and Asheville, NC. Some of the nation's most visited parks and forest areas are located in Southern Appalachia, including the Blue Ridge Parkway and the Great Smokey Mountain National Park.

While Appalachian scholars recognize the shared economic conditions in these three regions and similarities in way of life stemming from a lack of resources, most general studies about Appalachian people and culture focus on the more homogeneous population residing below the Mason-Dixon line, that is, what ARC designates as Central and Southern Appalachia. It is this area that is emphasized in the following.

Racial and Cultural Diversity

The Appalachian region was originally populated, of course, by indigenous Native Americans. By the time of European contact, tribal groups in the southeastern United States were extensive in number and had achieved a high level of social organization. It is estimated that as many as 60,000 Indians lived in the Appalachian mountains at the time of contact. As in other areas of the New World, these native populations were decimated soon after discovery due to warfare, forced labor, and disease. The discriminatory policies of the US government in the 18th and 19th centuries, and the forced removal of many groups, such as the Cherokee on the Trail of Tears to Oklahoma, resulted in further population declines. Today, relatively few Native Americans live in Appalachia. The Qualla Boundary in North Carolina, principal reservation of the Eastern Band of Cherokee Indians, has the largest concentration with a contemporary population of 11,500. In some areas, pockets of mixed-blood peoples of Indian-African-European heritage remain, such as the Melungeons in eastern Tennessee. Their origin and racial classification continue to be problematic (Beaver and Wilson 1997).

African Americans have been present in the mountains since the 1500s, brought first as slaves of Spanish and French explorers (Cabbell 1985). The mountains of Appalachia offered refuge for small numbers of freedmen and escaped slaves before the Civil War, and it was through mountain routes that the Underground Railroad transported thousands of runaway slaves to northern ports and Canada during the mid-1800s. Slavery, of course, was present in the mountains, but there is evidence that its character was unique (Inscoe 1989). Due to the absence of a plantation system of agriculture in the mountains, slaves were less numerous than in other parts of the south. Appalachian homesteads were relatively small, subsistence-based family farms with little need for a large labor force, and, in fact, only about 10% of the households in Appalachia held slaves. Where slaves were owned, they were often used in non-agricultural labor, as hotel servants or blacksmiths, and they were given somewhat more freedom in their movements than slaves in the plantation South. They were often household slaves, sharing living accomodations with the master's family. There is some evidence, perhaps due to these unique conditions of slavery, that white attitudes towards blacks were less prejudiced during this period in Appalachia than elsewhere in the Deep South (Cabbell 1985).

Following Emancipation, the demand for coal miners far exceeded the supply in Kentucky, Tennessee, Virginia, and West Virginia, and consequently there was a major migration of blacks from Alabama and, to a lesser extent, Mississippi. In 1860, only about 15,000 blacks lived in Central Appalachia. But by 1920 almost 90,000 blacks worked in the coal fields, and 69% of them resided in West Virginia where the full range of Jim Crow laws had never been enacted, in contrast to neighboring Appalachian states (Lewis 1987). Blacks chose to work in the Appalachian coal mines for sound economic reasons. As Ronald Lewis states, "Blacks not only were welcomed in the mountain coalfields, they were given equal wages for equal work and as good an opportunity in the occupational hierarchy as they were likely to find anywhere in industrial America" (1987:143). Certainly the life of a miner was difficult, but it was equally difficult for blacks and whites. Socially, however, blacks remained segregated in almost all coal company towns, where they had their own neighborhoods, recreational facilities, company-sponsored baseball teams, and schools.

The mines also attracted eastern and southern European immigrants, particularly from Italy, Hungary, Poland, Russia, and Czechoslovakia, as well as northern European immigrants from England, Germany, and Scotland. Lewis (1987) finds that coal mine operators pursued a policy of "judicious mixture" to ensure that their labor force was composed of a combination of African-Americans, native whites, and foreign workers. Reducing the social force of any one ethnic group was meant to "divide and conquer" in order to achieve maximum control over labor and to minimize the costs of production. In an arena in which power was so thoroughly dominated by the coal interests, however, workers instead forged a class movement characterized by ethnic and racial cooperation. The United Mine Workers of America (UMWA), established in 1890, offered union membership to all workers and a democratic alternative to the organization of their work. Black miners were equally active in the UMWA, which included participation in the bloody strikes of the 1920's and 30's. With the mechanization of coal production from the 1930's to the 1950's, however, hundred's of thousands of miners lost their livelihoods. Black miners were most affected by the changes and, by 1970, fewer than 4,000 remained in the industry (Lewis 1987).

Today, black Appalachians constitute approximately 8% of the region's population, and they have been more affected by the processes of out-migration and urbanization than white Appalachians. Blacks in the region suffer from severe socioeconomic deprivation, with the result that poverty is higher here than that for blacks nationally. William Turner summarizes their condition by saying, "The only group of persons worse off economically than black Appalachians are rural blacks in the United States. Rural Appalachian blacks are likely among America's poorest people" (1985b:257). Although little social research exists on black communities in the region, there is evidence that black Appalachians share a distinctive identity as "black" and "Appalachian," and that this sets them apart from other African-Americans in the US. Turner states that as such, black Appalachians are "a racial minority within a cultural minority" (1985a:xix).

The Europeans who came to mine coal from the 1890's to the 1920's also contributed to the religious diversity in the region. Most eastern and southern Europeans were Catholics, and priests followed them into the mountains to establish parishes. Many of the immigrants later migrated to northern cities with the increasing elimination of mining jobs in the 1930's, so the Catholic Church moved to establish missions in mountain county seats and to conduct "radio preaching" in order to stem the decline of Catholicism (Wolfe 1980). Other Europeans moved into the mountains in the 20th century to find permanent homes for themselves and their families. Many of these immigrants were peddlers, merchants, restauranteurs and other small business operators, and skilled craftsmen such as shoemakers and tailors. Small Jewish communities grew up in larger towns and cities in Appalachia, and occasional synagogues were founded.

Ethnic diversification continues to affect the Appalachian region. With the end of the Viet Nam War, a number of Hmong communities were established in rural areas through the missionary efforts of local churches. Changing agricultural labor demands have introduced new ethnic groups. With the growth of the Christmas tree industry in western North Carolina, for example, Hispanic farm workers (particularly Mexicans and Central Americans) have come to reside in the region.

Despite this ethnic diversity, the vast majority of Appalachian people (more than 80%) are descendents of northern European settlers who arrived in the region in the 18th and early 19th centuries. Immigrants to the ports of Pennsylvania during this period in American history were largely Scottish, English, Irish, and German, with small numbers of Welsh Baptists, Swiss Protestants, and French Huguenots (Fischer 1989). Facing conflict with the Quakers already settled in the vicinity of Philadelphia and Newcastle, these immigrants soon were pushed southward along the Atlantic coast into the Carolina piedmont and to the southwest into the Valley of Virginia along the Shenandoah River. They were encouraged by officials to move into the "back parts" of the colonies where they would form a buffer between the seaboard settlements and the Indians. The German immigrants tended to concentrate in the northern end of the Valley of Virginia and in Pennsylvania, becoming known as "Pennsylvania Dutch" (a derivative of Deutsch). From the Greater Appalachian Valley, the remaining immigrants migrated to the headwaters of smaller rivers in the Blue Ridge Mountains, and finally spilled across the Appalachian divide into the Allegheny Mountains of Kentucky and Tennessee. The region was largely settled by 1850, and later American immigrants began to by-pass the mountains, moving through the Ohio River Valley into the newly acquired western territories. No more large-scale migrations into the Southern Highlands occurred after the mid-nineteenth century, until the recent influx of newcomers connected with the tourist and recreation economy of the late twentieth century.

The vast majority (perhaps four-fifths) of the early European immigrants to Appalachia were Scotch-Irish (Campbell 1921), over 250,000 of them having arrived before the American Revolution. The Scotch-Irish were something of a hybrid group bound together mainly by religion and political economy (Fischer 1989). They were Calvanists, originally from the Scottish lowlands and the north of England, who were forced to emigrate to northern Ireland after it was claimed by England in the early 17th century. In Ulster, they continued to be exploited by high rents, low wages, and heavy taxes imposed by an Anglican elite and a Catholic majority. Joined by Irish Protestants who were also seeking religious and political freedom, many moved on to America. Free land in the western territory after the American Revolution attracted the settlers to the Appalachian mountains, but they were also impressed with the beauty of the land, the rich forests, the plentiful rivers and springs, and moderate temperatures. Scotch-Irish immigration peaked in the late 18th century and faded by the mid-nineteenth century. By this time, nonetheless, the Scotch-Irish had imposed their own distinctive cultural imprint.

In <u>Albion's Seed</u> (1989), historian David Hackett Fischer argues that the ethnic heritage of these settlers in the Appalachian region was sufficiently distinctive to create a different American regional culture he calls "Borderlands/Backcountry." Citing differences in 26 folkways, including speech, family, gender, death rituals, magic and religion, and conceptions of order, power, and freedom, Fischer contrasts the Borderlands/Backcountry subgroup with three others of British origin: the Puritans of New England, the southern English who settled in Virginia, and the North Midland English and Welsh of the Delaware Valley. Fischer points out that many of the Scotch-Irish continued to migrate within the United States, moving into Arkansas (the Ozarks) and Texas in the nineteenth century and to Arizona and southern California in the twentieth century.

Despite this historical pattern of migration and concentration in the Appalachian region, the Scotch-Irish as such have not maintained much of an ethnic identity in the US. As a result, there is little consensus on the contemporary nature of the Scotch-Irish as an ethnic group, nor do scholars regard this group as being relatively significant among Euro-American ethnic groups. For example, few references are ever made to the Scotch-Irish as a contemporary American ethnic group in the scholarly literature. On one hand, this is an extension of the tendency (until recently) not to recognize Euro-American ethnic groups as such in ethnicity texts. On the other hand, even among Euro-American groups, the Scotch-Irish are relatively obscure in the literature. In a recent study, I reviewed 20 general ethnicity texts that discussed European American ethnic groups, and found that the most commonly cited groups included Jewish, Irish, Italian, German, English, and Polish Americans (Keefe 1992). Each of these groups were cited in 12 or more of the books and were cited on at least 3% or more of the total pages in these books. The Scotch-Irish, on the other hand, were cited in only 8 of the books and on less than 1% of the total pages. Difficulty in establishing the character of the contemporary Scotch-Irish is increased by the fact that the US Bureau of the Census and most large-scale surveys treat the Scotch-Irish not as a single ethnic group but as an ethnic mixture of Scottish and Irish peoples (Alba 1990:342).

As a people, the Scotch-Irish have a weak identification with their European heritage. Despite being predominantly Scotch-Irish, for example, Appalachians rarely acknowledge their national origins (Beaver 1986), identifying more often simply as "Americans" or as "mountain" or "country" people. In many instances, they identify most with a state, county, or community locale. Mary Waters (1990) notes that the tendency to abstain from identifying with a Euro-American ancestry in the US is found most often among rural Southern whites with comparatively little education, those who might be expected, in fact, to have Scotch-Irish background.

According to the 1990 census, only 2.3% of the US population (5,617,713 people) claim Scotch-Irish ancestry, compared to 13.1% claiming English, 15.6% Irish, and 23.3% German ancestry (US Bureau of the Census 1992). Another 5% of the US population identify their ethnicity as "American," while 10.5% do not report ancestry. There are almost as many people who claim Scotch-Irish ancestry in California and Texas (1,042,382) as in the Appalachian states of West Virginia, Virginia, Kentucky, Tennessee, North Carolina, and Georgia (1,173,584). At the same time, almost three times as many people in these Appalachian states as compared to California and Texas claim "American" ancestry (3,606,051 vs. 1,539,560), and an even larger number does not report ancestry at all (4,985,223 vs. 4,251,509): that is, 29% of the population in these Appalachian states claim "American" identity or eschew ethnic ancestry altogether.

The above suggests a loss of a sense of Scotch-Irish identity, especially in the mountainous parts of these states. The reasons have to do, first, with the greater political utility of class and regional consciousness as opposed to Scotch-Irish ancestry among mountaineers as a means of organizing for resources. Royce (1982), Peterson (1980), and others have discussed the fact that ethnicity is a strategy for which individuals and groups may opt when it is advantageous in politically competitive situations. The relative isolation and homogeneity of the Appalachian population in the early 19th century would have reduced the need to enunciate a distinct heritage in competition for the plentiful resources in the region at the time. During the Civil War, mountain residents, who typically were not slave-owners, frequently sympathized with the Union's efforts and suffered political retaliation by southern state governments during and following Reconstruction. The late nineteenth century was also a period when wealthy northeastern capitalists began taking economic control of the land, mineral rights, timber reserves, and labor in the region. In other words, Appalachians were affected more by competition with other white residents in their states (many of whom were also Scotch-Irish) and with elite Euro-American Protestants who for the most part were absentee landlords. Regional and class identity were more reliable bases of organization for competition given these circumstances.

A second major reason for the loss of Scotch-Irish ethnicity involves the transformation of the Appalachian people as a result of their religious, political, and economic experience in America. The residents of the region were changed substantially by these processes, becoming a new people: they were no longer Presbyterians, nor simply subsistence farmers, nor even citizens in control of their own resources or destiny. These historical processes will be discussed in the next section.

A final aspect of diversity deserving mention is the increasing in-migration of non-Appalachians to the southern subregion. Appalachia in the twentieth century has been most characterized by out-migration due to economic deprivation, especially in the coal regions. With the rise of the tourism and recreation industry in southern Appalachia in the 1970's, many areas began to grow in population, because of the growing number of jobs. Some counties in western North Carolina, for example, such as Henderson and Watauga Counties, have increased in population by 20-40% since 1970.

In-migrants have often been Appalachian out-migrants returning home to begin again. More often, however, the in-migrants are newcomers attracted by the region's beautiful landscapes, rural lifestyle, and relative absence of urban problems such as crime, pollution, drugs, and traffic jams. Non-Appalachian newcomers hail from all parts of the country, but most often they come from nearby states or adjacent regions. In western North Carolina, for example, they are most frequently either from the Carolina piedmont or Florida. Some of the new arrivals, the "back to the landers," are urban ex-patriots seeking a simpler, less materialistic life (Beaver 1986). Others are wealthy second-home buyers, some of whom eventually become permanent mountain residents.

Given that they are generally white southerners in origin, newcomers often share a similar northern European heritage with mountaineers. Socially and culturally, however, they tend to be distinctive, as they are usually well-educated middle or upper middle class whites with urban backgrounds and more mainstream American lifestyles (Keefe, Reck, & Reck 1989). More and more frequently, they have come into conflict as a group with native Appalachians, particularly over land-use issues, such as zoning, and the legislation of moral codes, such as the sale of alcohol (Keefe 1994). As their numbers and political power grow, non-Appalachian residents will increasingly become a force to be reckoned with in certain parts of the Appalachian region. And as a consequence of their presence, native Appalachian residents can be expected increasingly to identify as an "ethnic group" in the region in order to try to secure their status in the new social order.

An Appalachian Ethnic Group?

While the region of Central and Southern Appalachia is racially and culturally diverse, it is nonetheless possible to speak of Appalachians as an ethnic group, or perhaps more accurately an "emerging ethnic entity" (Peterson 1980). The historical roots of this sense of identity are complex, yet the tendency to identify as "Appalachian" is manifested in groups as diverse as the Cherokee in western North Carolina, blacks in the West Virginia coal fields, and white mountaineers in rural eastern Tennessee. Because whites predominate in the region, the following narrative focuses on them.

Prior to 1880, Appalachia consisted of small family farms that were largely self-sustaining, producing their own handicrafts and relying on only a handful of market goods (i.e. coffee, sugar, salt) that they could not produce themselves. The Scotch-Irish came to America with a rural culture based on a non-intensive form of farming called "forest farming." This is practiced in marginal areas with poor soils where it is necessary to rotate cultivated plots frequently with forested areas (Blethen 1994). Livestock (hogs, cattle, and sheep) were also raised and allowed to graze freely on the acorn and chestnut mast on the forest floor. Hunting, fishing, and foraging wild plant foods (herbs, berries, nuts, and greens) were important economic pursuits. Original land grants in the mountains were relatively small, a few hundred acres at most, certainly a great deal smaller than those granted in the plantation region of the Deep South, and inheritance practices subdivided these family plots with each generation.

Nineteenth-century mountain communities were not the town-square New England variety, but rather formed "open-country neighborhoods" made up of intricate dispersed networks of family, friends, and neighbors within a common geographic location (along a hollow or a creek) and joined together by a shared history and moral code (Beaver 1986; Pearsall 1966). Schools, country stores, post offices, and churches, the typical anchors of rural community life, were uncommon until after 1890. Mountain communities were egalitarian and unstratified for the most part, each adult male being essentially a subsistence farmer. As in any rural agrarian society, economic exchange was based on reciprocity, or the exchange of goods and services between equals. Reciprocal exchange was epitomized by such traditional communal farming activities as barn-raisings, corn shuckings, and quilting parties.

The fundamental basis for membership in mountain society was kinship. This provided an idiom for conceiving social relationships, the concept of "equality" ultimately being based on the recognition of common blood heritage. As a real social system, kinship was the basis for most interaction as mountaineers lived and worked primarily within the extended family. In the absence of local churches and ministers, even religion tended to be family-based, fed by brief contact with circuit-riding preachers.

A series of religious revival movements, known as the Great Awakening, swept through the American colonies in the eighteenth century, and the Appalachian mountains and the rest of the South felt the impact of the second of these movements from about 1790 to 1810. The movement emphasized revivalism which involved frontier camp meetings, outdoor religious services, and emotional forms of preaching. The structure of the worship service permitted greater participation by the congregation than was usual in the established religions, and revivalism emphasized the individual religious experience rather than the religious doctrines of a particular church. The effect of the revival movement was to convert large numbers of people away from the orthodox religions.

The movement appealed to the Scotch-Irish and others who had been at odds with both the Church of England and political authoritarianism. It formed the basis of later evangelical Protestantism and the belief that individuals might be "born again" and, through faith, find everlasting salvation. At the heart of the religious movement was the personal conversion experience, the idea that every individual could personally find God and be saved. This was an optimistic frontier religion in contrast to traditional Calvinist beliefs in "divine election" and predestination. The new religious movement focused attention on the individual, the adherence to a personal code of moral ethics (including prohibitions against smoking, drinking, swearing, and gambling), and the expectation that people will respond vocally and emotionally when Jesus enters their hearts. Services became characterized by emotional expressiveness, as male and female participants responded to sermons with singing, shouting, and testifying and ended services with warm and friendly hugs, handshakes, and kisses (Dorgan 1987). The emphasis on a "literal" interpretation of the Bible meant that formal theological training (as demanded by the Presbyterian order, for example) was perceived as less important than receiving a "spiritual calling" to the word of God. So mountaineers welcomed the less educated farmer-preacher and emphasized religious "ordinances" following Christ's teachings and practices (such as creek baptisms and footwashing, an extension of the Lord's Supper) as opposed to religious "sacraments" emerging from formal church traditions (such as holy orders and church-sanctioned marriage).

A result of the Great Awakening was an increased religiosity among mountain people combined with a decline in affiliation with national church hierarchies. Today, the United Presbyterian Church as well as other mainline churches have little strength in rural parts of the region, which are dominated by small, family-based churches, usually Baptist, Methodist, or Holiness-Pentecostal. Church members' sentiments were not universally favorable to revivalism or related practices, such as Sunday school classes, causing many divided congregations and denominations. "Old Regular" Baptists, a highly traditional subdenomination largely located in Central Appalachia, for example, grew out of the contingent of Baptists rejecting revivalism (Dorgan 1989). In Appalachia, these divisions resulted in the emergence of numerous sectarian and independent churches, unaffiliated with national or "mainline" churches such as the Southern Baptist Convention or the United Methodist Church (although Appalachian churches were sometimes drawn together into loose "associations"). Humphrey (1984), for example, counts 47 varieties of Baptists in the mountains, 33 varieties of Methodists, and 18 varieties of Presbyterians. Mountain counties today are characterized by large numbers of simple, unassuming churches, typically having less than one-hundred members, scattered throughout the countryside. In a study of one rural county with a population of less than 35,000 in western North Carolina, for instance, 125 active churches were identified (Keefe et al. 1985).

The Great Awakening, then, served to loosen white southern highlanders' religious ties to their European homeland. Black Appalachians, like other black southerners, were also transformed by this spiritual movement and their religious practices and organization also reflect a preference for emotional rituals, revivalism, and sectarianism (Williams 1982).

Fifty years later the Civil War served to magnify the differences between the yeoman mountain farmers and the plantation aristocracy of the lowland South, furthering regionalism in Appalachia. As previously mentioned, slavery was less important in the mountains where the vast majority of whites were small landholders without the need or wherewithal to buy slaves. Throughout the nineteenth century, the mountainous parts of the southern states were often at odds with flatland rivals in statewide political battles in which the politically-dominant plantation owners generally were victorious. Economic ties of the mountain mercantile class (those most likely to be slaveowners) generally were with the South once the War Between the States broke out (Inscoe 1989), but sentiments varied among other mountaineers, many of whom joined the Union at the same time that others joined the Confederate forces. In addition, there were the "Tories," those with split loyalties who avoided enlisting in either army and who fled to the hills as "outliers" when they were in danger of being conscripted (Blackmun 1977). In certain mountain counties, the majority of sentiment was Unionist, and following the war these counties became Republican partisan strongholds, further distancing themselves from the Democratic majority in postbellum southern states (McKinney 1986).

These divided loyalties during the Civil War politically severed mountaineers from their southern compatriots. Hill people became stereotyped in state legislatures as backwards and undeserving of citizenship and equal rights, thus justifying the states' neglect of mountain roads and schools. Severe socioeconomic deterioration in the mountains was the result in the late nineteenth century.

The industrial development of Appalachia beginning around 1880 produced further radical transformations. Railroads began to be constructed with federal government subsidies, and by 1930 they criss-crossed the entire region leaving only a few counties without access (Eller 1982). The railroads were vital to the extraction of Appalachia's natural resources, especially timber and minerals, such as mica, iron ore, and coal, which had to be hauled to cities and markets where secondary industries converted them into goods and where consumers were available to buy them. Mining and timber companies began purchasing land and mineral rights, so that by 1900 many mountain counties had seen outside capitalists buy up a majority of these natural resources. Speculators often used unethical practices to buy and sell land. They also used such mechanisms as the "broad form" deed which made it possible, later, for the owners of mineral rights to engage in strip mining and, to destroy land that was owned by local mountaineers. The inevitable rising taxes that accompanied industrialization and the need for money in an increasingly market-driven rather than subsistence-based economy forced farmers to sell out or at least to take on wage labor to supplement their household incomes. The federal government also began to condemn and buy land as the National Park system (the backbone of modern tourism in Appalachia) took shape in the early twentieth century. By 1920, two brief generations following the penetration of capitalism, only 20% of the labor force in Appalachia was practicing fulltime farming.

Appalachia is often portrayed as a premodern, nonindustrial region, but in fact the area has long been industrialized, and indeed it provided much of the raw materials fueling American economic development during the twentieth century. What does set Appalachia apart from the rest of the country, on the other hand, is the character of its economic development as a peripheral region providing labor and natural resources to the core of the country, which skims off the profits by marketing those resources (Walls 1978). Appalachia lacked an intermediate stage of commercial transformation in the nineteenth century (Pudup 1990). This was due to a number of reasons, including a relatively homogeneous subsistence economy based on small, self-sufficient household farms with few transportation or production ties to external markets. When outside markets began to demand the timber and coal that the region contained, the capital required to exploit those resources had to come from outside investors also. And so, unlike the northeast where a slow evolution of capitalism and indigenous commercialization promoted the emergence of a substantial middle class and a local base of capital, Appalachia was "invaded by mature capitalist institutions" which converted the local population rather suddenly and almost wholly into working class laborers (Billings, Blee, & Swanson 1986). Moreover, the nature of the industries that took root in the region did not require a sophisticated labor force, and management actually benefitted from the perpetuation of a monoeconomy which forced workers to accept undesirable jobs for low pay. As a consequence, modernization and industrialization in Appalachia did not result in a rising standard of living but instead produced one of the highest rates of poverty in the country.

Many of the problems that Appalachia experiences in catching up economically with the rest of the nation today are rooted in this early industrial period when the ownership of basic resources passed from local to absentee ownership and the region became an "internal colony" controlled and exploited by outside interests (Lewis et al. 1978). The Appalachian Land Ownership Task Force (1983) found that in 1980 three-quarters of the surface land rights and four-fifths of the mineral rights in Appalachia are in the hands of absentee owners, mostly large, private (and multinational) corporations as well as federal government agencies (such as the Park Service and Forest Service). Local governments have inadequate monies for local development because federal lands are tax-exempt while private corporations benefit from lucrative tax breaks. Moreover, the extractive industries of the region do not promote the development of an economic infrastructure of roads, health clinics, good schools, and public services that would make the region attractive to a more diverse industrial base.

The historical experience of Appalachians has served to make a heterogeneous racial and cultural aggregate of people into a regional group with a shared identity. Caught up in the Great Awakening, Appalachians, like many other Americans, transformed their orientation from the Old World to the New World. Presbyterianism and Scotch Irish ethnicity lost strength as southern highlanders adapted to new cultural and environmental situations, in which regional residence and social class membership became important determinants of status in society. Links of political and economic geography to the rest of the South were fractured by the Civil War, so that Appalachian areas became, and remain, the "untended backyards" of southern states. Perhaps most importantly, Appalachia was transformed in a few brief decades around the turn of the century from a Jeffersonian frontier society to a highly stratified one in which the vast majority of native mountain residents became exploited laborers in a peripheralized region. These processes set the stage for an emerging consciousness among Appalachians as a people with a single historical experience, a shared relationship to the outside world, and a common destiny. Appalachian ethnic awareness was promoted by the images developed as others came to confront mountaineers at home and outside the hills.

The Construction of Cultural "Otherness"

It is perhaps no coincidence that at the same time industrialization and peripheralization of the Appalachian region was taking place in the late nineteenth century, an image of Appalachia as a "strange land and peculiar people" began to emerge in the American consciousness. Henry Shapiro (1978:x) argues that "the idea that the mountainous portions of eight or nine southern states form a coherent region inhabited by an homogeneous population possessing a uniform culture" was an invention of those from outside the region who came to perceive Appalachians as deviant from the American norm. The peculiarities identified as "Appalachian" contributed to their further estrangement from other white Protestants, other southerners, and other agrarian peoples in the nation. The growing perception of Appalachian cultural deviance served in many ways to justify the process of dispossession of their land and resources during the new era of capitalism. Moreover, the perception of an Appalachian "problem" fueled literary, missionary, and scholarly work, the popular media, and governmental policy for the next century.

Appalachia was "discovered" by the nation in the late nineteenth century on the pages of American magazines and books of fiction. A literary period now known as the "local-color movement" flourished following the divisive Civil War. Describing little-known places and people in picturesque styles, often as travel sketches and short stories laced with dialect, local color writers provided middle-class readers of Scribner's, The Atlantic Monthly, and Harper's Magazine with a vision of national unity through symbolic contrast with the "other." Appalachia and other remote areas of the country were exploited for their geographic wonders, biological curiosities, and cultural peculiarities thought to be of interest to readers in eastern cities. Fiction writers, such as Mary Noailles Murfree (In the Tennessee Mountains 1884) and John Fox, Jr. (The Little Shepherd of Kingdom Come 1903; The Trail of the Lonesome Pine 1908), dealt with dramatic "confrontations between characters emblematic of the two cultures--feudists and lawmen, moonshiners and revenue officers, dirt-farmers and mining engineers, plain folks and politicians, mountain girls and city boys" (Shapiro 1978:20). The earlier, romantic notion of Daniel Boone-style pioneers of mountain stock was replaced by unappealing images of Appalachians as anarchists, criminals, rubes, degenerates, and victims. These stereotypic images were to be reinvigorated by the popular media of the twentieth century.

In another post-Civil War development, Protestant missionaries sent by northern churches entered the mountains as part of an aggressive evangelization and Americanization of the South. As Shapiro points out, "The local-color writers saw Appalachia as an 'unknown' land because they had never been there. In the same way, the home missionaries of the northern Protestant churches saw Appalachia as an 'unchurched' land because their denominations were not represented there" (1978:32). By the mid-1880's, all northern Protestant churches (including Presbyterian, Episcopalian, Methodist, Congregational, and Quaker) had missionaries working among southern whites. In addition to ministerial practice, benevolent work in the southern mountains primarily consisted of establishing schools and churches. These were the institutions perceived both as absent and as critical in addressing the social as well as geographic "isolation" of mountain people caught in "Rip Van Winkle sleep". Mary Noailles Murfree's In the Tennessee Mountains was used as a text to inform new missionaries about the region. Going beyond the local-color definition of mountain life as distinctive and degenerate, however, denominational workers found in Appalachia a social problem and the need for uplifting a people not so much degraded as "not yet graded up." The establishment of mission churches, mission schools, and colleges institutionalized the acceptance of Appalachian otherness.

Berea College in Berea, Kentucky, was founded in 1855 as part of the missionary movement in the mountains. One of the most influential presidents of Berea College, William Goodell Frost, was the first to name the region, known in the nineteenth century only as "the central South." In an essay written for Atlantic Monthly in 1899 entitled "Our Contemporary Ancestors in the Southern Mountains," Frost revealed the architecture of his vision of the region he called "Appalachian America," a region of mountainous terrain in the heart of the most civilized area of the nation, a region in which a hardy race of pioneers continued to live in traditional ways. By naming it, Frost gave Appalachia a sense of coherence and homogeneity not otherwise apparent (Shapiro 1978). By referring to mountaineers as the nation's "ancestors," Frost conceded Appalachia's backwardness while at the same time urging national concern about the people who were, he argued, close kin of mainstream whites.

Benevolent workers were attracted to the southern mountains in the hopes of providing both their version of the gospel and a sense of community which was thought to be necessary for social progress. The perceived "absence of community" in the mountains was believed to be a consequence of isolation. The outbreak of feuds around the turn of the century, especially in Kentucky, West Virginia, and Tennessee, confirmed emerging notions that Appalachians were stubbornly independent, anti-social, and lawless. Journalists' descriptions of family feuds and related murder trials were eagerly consumed by readers of eastern newspapers. Some social historians assert that feuding was customary among mountaineers, who brought a tradition of autonomous family retribution for wrongdoing from northern Britain (Fischer 1989). In a careful investigation of the famous Hatfield and McCoy feud, however, Altina Waller (1988) finds a better explanation in the invasion of the mountains by industrial capitalism and the development of economic inequality in what had been a kin-based, egalitarian culture. "Devil Anse" Hatfield was, in fact, an ambitious local entrepreneur who in 1877 started a timber company employing 30 men, including many family members; while "ol' Ranel" McCoy and his sons, who were landless, had a more marginal standing. The twelve year feud beginning in 1878 engaged old family animosities in a changing economic climate where competitors were not only outside vested interests but indigenous market capitalists.

The settlement movement came to Appalachia at the turn of the century to bring social and cultural development to a people perceived as lacking both. Part of the larger settlement house movement (whose best known example is Jane Addams' Hull House in Chicago), various rural settlements were established in the southern mountains by young women, graduates of northern colleges such as Smith and Bryn Mawr, who were called to the Victorian ideal of "social guardianship" (Whisnant 1983). Settlement schools were meant to "revive" local culture, especially handicraft traditions, among the adult population, but the crafts also reflected outside influences brought in by the outsiders themselves, including new weaving patterns and woodworking styles (Whisnant 1983). Settlement school directors also imported and taught their own version of proper cooking, housekeeping, and even silverware table settings, as well as new ways of celebrating holidays such as Christmas, and new forms of socializing on Saturday nights (foregoing moonshine drinking and raucous dancing for more genteel rituals).

Folk schools, introduced at the same time as rural settlement schools, were more specifically intended to provide self-sustaining economic alternatives for mountaineers through the "perpetuation" of local traditions. They, too, however, more often resulted in cultural invention and manipulation. The most well-known folk school, the still extant John C. Campbell Folk School in Brasstown, North Carolina, for example, was founded on the Danish School model and even incorporated Danish folksongs and dances into the curriculum. David Whisnant (1983) points out that these intentional and systematic cultural interventions were part of a "politics of culture" in which non-Appalachians sought to shape the thoughts and values of mountaineers, with profound consequences for their identity and sense of cultural differentness.

Coincident with the founding of folk schools in the mountains was the labeling of Appalachians as "folk," or a separate people with a "folk culture." In one sense, this was meant to justify the establishment of folk schools which assumed the pre-existance of a crafts tradition which might be preserved through the school curriculum. It also lent a sense of the "primitive" to the products produced and marketed by mountain men and women, such as quilts, knotted bed canopy fringes, coverlets, rag carpets, oak-splint baskets, brooms, split-bottomed chairs, wooden toys, and handmade dulcimers and banjos. The handicraft movement in Britain and America at the turn of the century brought recognition to the aesthetic merit of "naif" work and helped to foster an economic market for handmade crafts. Folk school directors were quick to exploit the commercial advantages for mountain people who were promoted as "the conservators of our common Anglo-Saxon heritage, preservers of the folk culture of Merrie Olde England and the individualism of the days of the pioneers" (Shapiro 1978:218).

Efforts to preserve traditional folksongs and folkdances followed in the footsteps of the crafts "revival" movement. Olive Dame Campbell, the wife of John C. Campbell, was one of the early folk ballad collectors in the mountains. At her urging, Cecil J. Sharp, a well-known British collector of folksongs, arrived in 1916 and worked with singers in North Carolina and Tennessee. Sharp was impressed with the quality of his informants whom he characterized as "just English peasant folk [who] do not seem to me to have taken on any distinctive American traits. They talk English, sing English, behave English!" (quoted in Whisnant 1983:116). The collaborative efforts of Campbell and Sharp produced a joint publication, <u>English Folk Songs of the Southern Appalachians</u> (1917). Like other Appalachian collections published in the period, special emphasis was put on folksong "survivals," including ballads such as "Barbara Allen,"

"Pretty Polly," "Young Edward," and "Lord Daniel's Wife." This enchantment with the persistence of English folk culture was echoed in the delight of settlement school directors who discovered "Elizabethan" speech patterns in the mountains. At Hindman Settlement School in eastern Kentucky, for example, children were even taught Shakespearean plays in order to employ their supposedly natural "Elizabethan" dialect, with less than satisfactory results (Whisnant 1983).

Where English survivals were absent, settlement schools sometimes introduced them. One of the most arresting examples of this involves morris dancing, believed to be a form of "ancient pan-European seasonal pagan observances associated in some way with fertility" (Whisnant 1983). Disturbed by his failure to find morris or related sword-dance ceremonies in the southern mountains, Cecil Sharp began to teach them to mountain people at Hindman and Pine Mountain Settlement Schools in Kentucky immediately following his arrival. When mountain folk festivals celebrating traditional music became popular in the 1930's, such as White Top Folk Festival in Virginia, they served as venues for the further preservation of these "reintroduced" dance forms.

Mountain music was reshaped even more dramatically for a mainstream American market with the influence of the commercial music industry. As early as 1923, mountain musicians were producing phonograph recordings with impressive commercial success, and the record industry adopted the name of an early group from Galax, Virginia, the "Hill Billies," to refer to the entire musical genre (Tribe 1990). The most significant musical group to emerge from the southern mountains during this early period, the Carter Family, included in their repertoire all of the diverse traditions in Appalachian songmaking: British and traditional American ballads, nineteenth century popular and Victorian songs, sacred lyrics and gospel music, and African American and minstrel show songs. Later artists from the mountains were encouraged to stray from these traditions and to write their own songs to appeal to a wider commercial market, and new musical styles were created, such as Bluegrass music in the 1940's which modernized "old-time" string band music. Radio shows, such as the Grand Ol' Opry, popularized music that became known as "country and western," in which the country or mountain music oftentimes had to adopt a semi-comic, dialect-peppered style in order to gain acceptance. Television versions of these shows, such as "Hee Haw" (which enjoys great popularity in the rural south), perpetuate the humorous and often negative connotations of the hayseed trappings used to characterize mountain culture.

The "hillbilly" stereotype emerging in the music industry has been echoed in other commercial media throughout the twentieth century. Cartoonists, such as Paul Webb drawing for Esquire (1935-1948), Al Capp who created "Li'l Abner" in 1934, and Fred Lasswell who draws "Snuffy Smith," have used mountain images to communicate themes of ignorance, poverty, sloth, filth, immorality, and regressive attitudes and behaviors. Jerry Williamson (1995) demonstrates the significance of Appalachian themes in Hollywood productions beginning with early silent films to the Ma and Pa Kettle films of the 1940's and the popular "Beverly Hillbillies" television show of the 1960's, all of which projected familiar stereotypes both to the nation and to foreign audiences. Commoditization of these Appalachian images continues in the expanding tourism industry in the region, where "hillbilly" trading posts and "country" emporiums sell "outhouse" and moonshine-still replicas, 'coon dog portraits, and "chewing tobacco" chewing gum.

Since the late nineteen-hundreds, Appalachia has attracted considerable national attention. Images of Appalachian people and culture have been created and manipulated by those from outside the region to serve as examples of "otherness," from visions of hardy self-sufficient pioneers to isolated and lawless anarchists to romantic reminders of America's ethnic folk heritage to laughable rubes hopelessly out of place in modern America to a national social problem that must be solved. This "invention" of Appalachia, as Allen Batteau (1990) points out, is perhaps best understood as a consequence of various national concerns, including unification, modernization, and social progress. The images have had an impact on Appalachian peoples' identity, forcing them to deal with the pervasive negative stereotypes. But the images have little to offer in providing an accurate understanding of Appalachian culture and values. For this, we must turn to the ethnographic evidence and to community studies carried out in the region.

Appalachian Culture and Values

Ethnographers documenting Appalachian culture agree on a number of core values and cultural features. While most ethnographic studies of Appalachian communities concentrate on rural areas and very small towns, similar cultural traits are found in studies of Appalachian migrants to cities outside the region. It must be assumed that these traits are also characteristic of Appalachian residents in larger towns and cities within the region, although this awaits confirmation by future urban ethnographies.

Appalachian culture is not wholly unique, for it shares much with rural Southern culture and rural agrarian lifestyle in general, but as a pattern of ideas and expectations for behavior Appalachian culture is coherent and distinctive. The following attributes are essential to Appalachian culture: egalitarianism, independence and individualism, personalism, an avoidance of conflict, familism, a religious world view, and a sense of place.

Egalitarianism

Egalitarianism, of course, is an American cultural value. As Beaver (1986) explains, however, in Appalachia it has more significant "mythical" qualities as a guide for people's actions. Certainly mountain communities are stratified (although given the rural economy, status differences may not be as great nor as pervasive as in urban areas). But great effort is taken to ignore these differences in social relations. Common in mountain communities is the country store or small cafe where all members of the community, rich and poor, meet and greet one another by first names and sit down together at the same table or counter. Everyone expects to be treated with identical courtesy and to ask about each other's families. There is little pretense or status differentiation by dress in mountain communities, where everyone dresses informally and women wear little or no make-up (Hicks 1976). Conspicuous consumption is avoided. People in general are self-deprecating, often by joking about themselves (Miles 1975). Loyal Jones (1994) refers to this as the value of humility. Those who set themselves above others are referred to pejoratively as "getting above their raisin'," "uppity," or "big shots." Even community leaders seek to be self-effacing in the public eye. Mountaineers identify with "Jack" of the Jack-in-the-Beanstalk folk tales, where Jack through courage and intellect is able to outwit the giant and the fancy folk. Also like Jack, mountaineers may engage in petty theft or vandalism as sanctions against those in the community with condescending attitudes or pretensions of higher class (Beaver 1986).

One idiom for expressing this assumption of sameness is kinship. As Bryant (1981) points out, the commonly heard "We're all kin here" indicates that people in the mountains perceive themselves to be like one another, of the same flesh and blood. And non-kin are often incorporated into kinship networks as equals through the extension of kinship terms and obligations

Beaver 1986; Halperin 1990). Economic strategies in mountain communities are anchored on the family household and the value of adequacy (Halperin 1990). The goal is to make ends meet and provide for family needs, not to make profits. Halperin (1990) describes the "multiple livelihood strategies" used by rural families to adapt to the local mix of capitalist and precapitalist economies where reliance on a single livelihood would be risky. By using their land to plant subsistence gardens, working in factories as temporary wage labor, doing their own household repairs, bartering with neighbors and friends, patronizing flea markets where cheaper factory seconds and used goods are sold, and relying on kin networks to pool resources, mountain people resist dependency on capitalism and are able to maintain a traditional rural lifestyle. This lifestyle also reinforces homogeneity in the social community where no one is a specialist and everyone is relatively autonomous. And as Halperin (1990) points out, while this livelihood may result in low income, people do not think of their family as "poor." Instead, their ability to "make do" is held in high esteem within the local community (Stephenson 1968).

As the preferred form of economic exchange, reciprocity with family, friends, and neighbors also reinforces egalitarianism. Miles (1975) was struck by the extensive hospitality mountain people bestowed on visitors when she lived in eastern Tennessee during the late nineteenth century. Neighborliness is still highly valued and people are expected to repay "kindliness for kindliness" (Miles 1975). Mountain people like to come visiting with gifts of food or produce from their garden. The most common form of gathering is the "covered dish" dinner where all participants come together to share homemade foods. The food is plentiful but simple fare found on common tables and rooted in the people's subsistence heritage: plates of fried chicken, country ham biscuits, and country style steak; pots of chicken and dumplings and trays of deviled eggs; vegetable dishes such as green beans, pinto beans, corn on the cob, cole slaw, green salads, sliced cucumbers, and vine-ripened tomatoes; fresh fruit and fruit cobblers; cornbreads and other homemade varieties of bread; pies, cakes, and banana puddings; together with jugs of sweetened iced tea and Kool-Aid as well as pots of hot coffee. Music (also homemade) is often provided at these events and reinvokes the themes of simplicity and family, as individuals are taught to sing and play traditional pieces by close relatives and family members often come together to form musical groups (a pattern also found in professional Country music groups such as the Carter Family and the Statler Brothers).

Individualism and Independence

Like egalitarianism, individualism and independence are core American values that have special significance and distinctive manifestations for Appalachians. Whereas mainstream Americans interpret individualism as the right to non-conformity and equal opportunity to compete for the American Dream, Appalachians emphasize the aspects of sovereignty and self-reliance. This is captured in a story related by Loyal Jones:

> Several years ago there came a great snowfall in western North Carolina. The Red Cross came to help people who might be stranded without food or fuel. Two workers heard of an old lady way back in the mountains living alone, and they went to see about her, in a four-wheel drive vehicle. After an arduous trip they finally skidded down into her cove, got out and knocked on the door. When she appeared, one of the men said,
> "Howdy, ma'am, we're from the Red Cross," but before he could say anything else, the old lady replied,
> "Well, I don't believe I'm a-goin to be able to help you any this year. It's been a right hard winter." (Jones 1994:51)

The self-sufficient aspect of individualism is that which is admired in the pioneer past and glorified in Foxfire's Aunt Arie (Wigginton and Benett 1984). Social workers find that mountain people resist charity and social welfare programs despite possible need. Beaver (1986) finds the qualities of common sense, dependability, cooperation and, especially, hard work are the basis for an individual's sense of "worth" and respect in the community. Not working or living on public assistance or transgressing moral codes may result in being considered "worthless" and exclusion from the social community.

Children as young as five years old in rural Appalachia learn to take on tasks in the household and contribute to the family's livelihood (Beaver 1986). They are given increasing responsibility with age, particularly in farming families. Young boys are encouraged to use guns and begin to hunt by the time they are ten or twelve years old. Children, particularly boys, are allowed to be venturesome and are expected to take care of themselves with little supervision (Hicks 1976). This expectation of "unbounded personal freedom" echoes an ancestral dislike of authoritarianism and a tendency to "take care of our own" (Fischer 1989). It is sometimes expressed in a preference for solitude, as in the common pastimes of fishing and deer-stand hunting.

Sovereignty is sought in social as well as personal life. Mountaineers have a tradition of resisting governmental authority, as illustrated in the region's moonshining heritage. Using techniques brought from the British Isles, mountaineer entrepreneurs capitalized on Prohibition, turning low-profit corn into higher-profit corn liquor and running it to major cities outside the region, for the most part avoiding federal law until its production became less profitable in the 1950's. Halperin (1990) also finds widespread evidence of resistance in traits such as keeping the homeplace debt-free (and therefore beyond outside control) and omission of cash odd-jobs from income taxes. Beaver sees this mountain value of autonomy more generally:

> Independence, then, means "minding one's own business" or not meddling in other people's business and, at the same time, expecting to be left alone in managing one's own affairs. This concept is expressed most frequently in the simple phrase "Ain't nobody gonna tell me what to do." (Beaver 1986:153)

Appalachian individualism may be described as "cooperative independence" whereby people cooperate in order to preserve their autonomy and not as a form of anarchism which threatens social harmony (Stephenson and Greer 1983).

Personalism

Like Southerners in general, Appalachians appreciate and encourage personal face-to-face relations. Mountain people interact with others based on a recognition of their individuality. This is reflected in a story told by Helen Lewis in which she asks a young boy named Johnny what he will be when he grows up, and he says "I'll be Johnny" (Lewis et. al. 1978). Hicks (1976) remarks that personal status, based on family background, reputation, leisure pursuits, indebtedness, and personality, is something everyone has, like class status, although personal status may be more important! In many mountain counties, this personal status is reflected in the tendency to name roads after individuals. In Watauga County, NC, for example, 33% of the rural roads incorporate personal names, such as "Preacher Billings Road," "Moretz Family Farm Road," and "Julia Pearson Lane."

Mountain people are well-known for their friendliness and hospitality toward others. Weller (1965), for example, recounts a story about Peace Corps trainees from the University of Kentucky who were sent without money to hollers in eastern Kentucky and, by relying on the neighborliness of mountain people, were able to find food and shelter for a week without any trouble.

Mountaineers make eye contact with people when interacting, transforming even mundane economic transactions into personal ones. A local student of mine working at a supermarket in Boone, NC, remarked that she refused to begin ringing up each customer's purchases until the customer looked at her when she said "Hello." Social contact is also evident on the roadways, as drivers frequently honk, wave, or raise their hand or index finger in recognition of other drivers or pedestrians. Socializing in general is extremely important and marks all activities taking place in the community. Sherrod (1991) finds "fellowship" even more significant than ministerial activities among congregations in mountain churches. Churches typically have Wednesday night fellowship suppers, Homecoming Day honoring those who have moved away, and "dinners on the ground" in the summertime. Funeral services include a "visitation" the day before when family and friends come together, often in the home of the surviving relatives, to share personal support and intimate time together.

Honest and fair dealings make for strong personal ties among mountaineers, who are loyal to those they trust (Jones 1994). Verbal agreements are binding and do not require paper authorization. While mountaineers count on each other to keep their word, there is a general mistrust of government, institutions, and the rich (Stephenson 1968; Weller 1965). People work hard to be likable and accepted, and there are strong sanctions in the community if they stray. As Beaver notes, "gossip is in perpetual movement along complex and overlapping networks.... [It] provides the medium for expressing personal and collective evaluations of behavior and allows one to avoid face-to-face encounters" (Beaver 1986:162). For these reasons, privacy is keenly sought and protected. Families guard secrets in order to stay out of the gossip chains, often making it difficult for social workers, counselors, and other professionals to work openly with clients (Fiene 1994).

<u>Avoidance of Conflict</u>

Like Southerners in general, Appalachians tend to promote peaceful cooperation and avoid conflict in personal relations. To keep the peace, they do not make public pronouncements about someone or something they dislike. These opinions may be expressed privately, however, or as part of gossip controls. In fact, the common way an individual learns she or he has done something unacceptable is "through the grapevine" and not in a face-to-face encounter. This avoidance of hostile expression is learned at an early age. Preschoolers are encouraged to share and play in harmony rather than speak in anger (Kovarski and Braswell 1994). Aggressive, even authoritative, behavior is considered rude outside the family, and leadership roles are often rejected due to a concern that they might involve uncomfortable confrontations (Hicks 1976; Stephenson 1968). Successful leaders are able to avoid arguments and bring about consensus without offending others.

Social mechanisms to avoid conflict include the use of formal etiquette, giving indirect advice, couching reprimands with humor and jokes, and exhibiting a taciturn demeanor. There is a high regard for manners and etiquette as a means of avoiding personal offense. Mountaineers address others as "Sir" or "M'am" not to indicate high status but as a form of respect. Mountain people avoid giving advice directly to non-kin, preferring to introduce the topic indirectly by saying something like: "Now, if it were me,...." After a year of rancor and dissention in the high school in my county, a well-respected member of the community who had recently been stricken by cancer wrote a letter to the editor lamenting that he had not done more to prevent the school's problems, by implication asking what excuse others had for not taking action. George Hicks gives a good example of the way in which self-deprecating humor is often used to defuse situations and reinforce an "ethic of neutrality:"

> In a long discussion of county politics one afternoon,... Carmon Mitchell attempted to make a joke at his friend's expense by saying, "Ollis, why don't you run for jackass of Kent County?" Ollis puffed his pipe silently while the other men roared. Sensing that he had gone too far, Carmon added, "I'll just step down and let you take the office." (Hicks 1976:90)

Hicks (1976) also finds some truth to the widely noted "taciturnity" of mountain people, who perhaps wisely develop nonverbal and nonemotional responses to situations where others might be sensitive to insult, and Appalachians may suffer discrimination by cultivating these traits. For example, as a group they tend to score higher in pathology on the MMPI, a common psychological assessment tool, on the "social introversion" scale that tests for "increasing levels of social shyness, preference for solitary pursuits, and lack of social assertiveness" (Keefe, Hastrup, & Thomas 1993:5).

Cultural mechanisms for conflict resolution are available in mountain churches where footwashing and flower ceremonies are practiced. Footwashing commemorates the practice ordered by Christ when He washed His disciples' feet prior to the Last Supper, and involves all members of the congregation who move forward one by one to wash another's feet using a basin of water and a towel. Howard Dorgan describes the emotionally cathartic nature of this ceremony:

> ...one person finally decides to approach, basin in hand, the one church member for whom he or she holds the most antipathy, or that estranged family member toward whom profound bitterness has in the past been directed. These are the encounters that typically produce the highest drama and from which the most needed therapeutics may be derived. (Dorgan 1989:111)

Elsewhere, Dorgan (1987) describes a "Flower Service" in which church members bring home-grown bouquets and are urged to "Get right with thy neighbor" by exchanging flowers symbolic of forgiveness of old grudges and misunderstandings. He suggests that lasting anger is difficult to maintain with this kind of pressure for reconciliation. Yet, conflict is less easily resolved beyond the boundaries of a particular church or with newcomers unversed in mountain ways. Moreover, there are few cultural mechanisms for dealing with more overt hostility, and it can easily escalate beyond the point that it can be handled by normal mechanisms of social control.

Familism

The family is the fundamental social institution in Appalachia, and familism is the basis for the construction of social relations in general. The Appalachian family is structured somewhat differently than the mainstream American family: (1) the Appalachian family includes not just the nuclear family but an extended "family group" consisting of parents, their grown children, and their families, (2) individuals tend not to act alone but always to orient their behavior with reference to the family group, and (3) blood kinship is the strongest basis for social ties, superseding ties with friends, in-laws, or often, even spouses (Keefe 1988). As I have noted,

> Sometimes this results in interesting visiting patterns within the nuclear family. One woman I interviewed, for example, married into her husband's community. One of his brothers lives nearby and the brothers visit daily, often at her house. However, she says, she doesn't talk to her brother-in-law. Her concern is directed more toward her own "family," particularly her parents with whom she visits every Sunday. (Keefe 1988:26)

Socializing is done mostly (sometimes exclusively) with relatives. Holidays are always family-oriented, and additional rituals such as family reunions and Memorial Day gatherings in family cemeteries are commonplace in Appalachia. Rural mountaineers may be unfamiliar or ill-at-ease with forms of social organization requiring interaction with strangers and non-kin, such as the pervasive voluntary organizations of mainstream America (Hicks 1976; Stephenson 1968).

Community in Appalachia is anchored on kinship which provides the real social networks and the cultural values that bind people into community (Beaver 1986). And indeed households in the rural community are connected by blood or marriage. Siblings continue to maintain close ties into adulthood, and first cousins also tend to be especially close. Matthews (1965), for example, finds the naming of children follows collateral ties to cousins and siblings rather than lineal ties to parents or grandparents. Individuals may marry cousins, including first cousins, which strengthens the ties between collateral kin. Appalachian communities often have sets of "double cousins," or children of siblings who married siblings and, therefore, are related to each other by double bonds of kinship (Matthews 1965).

Economy in Appalachia is a family economy which is based on a relationship among kin who are associated with a specific plot of land (Beaver 1986; Halperin 1990). Land is passed down through the family, and it is land ownership that ultimately connects family members (Bryant 1981). Family often live on the same plot of land in Appalachia, and one common manifestation of this is the clustering of small homes and trailors housing family groups along country roads. Family members rely on one another for their well-being, exchanging goods and services and cooperating in organized activities such as gardening, farming, and house-building. The interdependence of kin networks and kin obligations is manifest in the political sphere as well, where family members' loyalty is expected in voting for agreed-upon candidates, and where a candidate, if elected, is expected to appoint kin to political offices (Hicks 1976).

Appalachians continue to honor family members after their death. This tradition contributes to an attitude of greater acceptance of death in Appalachia than in mainstream America, in which the denial of death is more pronounced (Sherrod 1990). Attendence at both the visitation preceding the funeral and the memorial service is expected of family and friends (Crissman 1994). Funeral processions cause other drivers to pull over spontaneously to the side of the road and stop while they pass, a pattern that is followed only sporadically for ambulances in my town! Deceased relatives are frequently memorialized through the newspaper publication of their pictures and special poems written by living relatives (often years or decades following the death), through Decoration (Memorial) Day cleaning of cemetary graves and placing of fresh flowers, and, as Dorgan notes, through reverential readings of deceased members names during church services.

Religious World View

Religion is pervasive in mountain life. Most mountain people identify as Christians and practice personal moral codes which are based on conservative interpretations of the Bible, and which disavow alcohol, gambling, and profanity. Even if they don't go to church, mountaineers enjoy reading and arguing about the Bible any day of the week (Humphrey 1984; Miles 1975). Prayer is also a part of daily life. Until recent Supreme Court rulings, prayers typically began civic meetings and important rites of passage, such as graduation. There is reliance on prayer for healing sickness (Keefe & Parsons 1996). Rural Appalachians favor country and gospel music, both of which incorporate religious themes and references. Weekly gospel programs are produced by small radio stations throughout the Southern Appalachian ranges (Dorgan 1987). Churches often have "singings" during the week when the congregation gathers for an hour or more in the evening to sing hymns and play religious tunes. During the summertime, singings may be held outside and provide a social as well as sacred occasion. A "Singing on the Mountain" is held each summer on Grandfather Mountain, NC, attracting 10,000 or more participants from near and far. A Trail of Tears Singing is held in Cherokee, NC, each June incorporating members of both Eastern and Western Cherokee who, through Christian music, remember the four thousand who died during the forced removal to Oklahoma in 1838-39 (Neely 1991).

Mountain religion expresses the cultural themes important to Appalachian people. Egalitarianism is manifested in the simple church buildings housing small, homogeneous congregations, led often by preachers with only high school degrees who are addressed not as "Pastor" but simply as "Brother so-and-so." Rituals such as creek baptism and footwashing teach humility and simplicity. Concern for individualism and personalism is found in the emphasis by the mountain church on personal salvation rather than on social works (Ford 1962). These values are reinforced during church services at times when the preacher singles out the personal sins of members to illustrate the need to follow Biblical commandments, or when the congregation joins in "oral prayer," each individual saying their personal prayer aloud at the same time as everyone else.

The church is typically conceptualized as a "family of Christ" (Bryant 1981). Fellow church members are all "Brothers and Sisters" who worship the Father. Cemeteries are maintained by those related to the dead, as Appalachian poet Robert Morgan reminds us in "Cleaning Off the Cemetery:"

> Not the church-devout but those
> reverent to family memory
> show for these workings held
> every three to five springs,
> some driving a ways, complaining,
> but always here on the chosen day
> with tools and kids and dinner.
> (Morgan 1987:52)

Familism is also evident in the congregations, which are typically made up of members bound by ties of social kinship, and in annual church "homecomings" which celebrate the reunion of actual kin groups as well as church members.

Sense of Place

Appalachian people have a strong sense that the mountains are home. While outsiders appreciate the southern highlands for aesthetic and economic reasons, mountain people have sacred attachments to the land that symbolizes family, livelihood, and ancestral roots. A man in southwest Virginia captures this sentiment:

> Land in this area doesn't change hands much. The place we live on has been in the family for seven generations. This is not real estate, this is home and will be handed down, I hope, for seven more generations. (Morefield 1990:63)

Mountaineers come to know their land not as a generic but as a specific piece of earth with landmarks and bits of local history that give it meaning (Hicks 1976). While newcomers feel compelled to leave the mountains occasionally in order to cope with the perceived isolation, mountain people love their land, enjoy showing it off and being on it. When asked where they would like go on a vacation, Wagner's (1995) informants in southwest Virginia frequently replied that they would like to take their vacation at home!

Those who migrate out of the mountains commonly complain of being homesick for the place as well as the people, and there are high rates of return migration as a result. A middle-aged woman from Mount Rogers, VA, reminisces:

> I moved away from here one time, up north to Baltimore. Now I know this is going to sound silly but -- when I would say my prayers at night it was like "God" wasn't there. I know that's crazy but that's the way it felt to me. It was because I wasn't in the mountains where I was supposed to be -- where I needed to be. (Morefield 1990:23)

Richard Humphrey finds this sense of the mountains as a sacred place particularly strong in deep rural areas where people are likely to practice what he calls the "religion of Zion," Zion being the mountainous place in the Old Testament referred to in Psalms 121:1-2: "I will lift up mine eyes unto the hills from whence cometh my help." Appalachian writers and poets often refer to this kinship with the land felt by mountain people, and perhaps none has captured it as well as James Still in the poem "Heritage" in which he declares that "Being of these hills I cannot pass beyond" (Still 1968:82). Writers from the coalfields, including Still (1940), Norman (1972), and Giardina (1987), typically incorporate in their novels a sense of longing for the land that has been stolen by the mining companies. The landscape is also evoked spiritually as when poet Robert Morgan states:

> Mountains speak in tongues. Take the wide thought of estuaries. The absent god leaves the forest and the tundra soaked in divinity. (Morgan 1978:42)

In mountain communities, this melding of the land, the Lord, and the people is accomplished each year when religious services are taken outdoors for baptisms, Decoration Day, and tent revivals.

Mountaineers feel the responsibility of stewardship toward the land and the need to make it productive while protecting and preserving it (Eller 1982). They hope to inherit land from their parents, to work it, and to pass it on to their children. Land becomes associated with families, and the "homeplace" where ancestors settled is kept in the family and is often the location of the family reunions. The homeplace includes not only the house but also the grounds and even the farmland of past generations. Land is essential to the maintenance of the "multiple livelihoods" of mountain families, and people struggle to keep their land, often commuting 50-100 miles a day to find wage labor (Halperin 1990). In this way, Appalachians are able to maintain the rural lifestyle they prefer while taking advantage of urban resources that are necessary.

Mountaineers identify with their community which is the integration of people and place. Typically, these are small locales where residents know one another and feel comfortable and secure. Mountain communities are unlikely to be listed on any maps of the area, which generally include only incorporated towns and county seats. In one study, 72 communities were identified in a single rural Appalachian county in North Carolina (Plaut, Landis & Trevor 1993). These included rural roads and hollars, family compounds, crossroads hamlets, river and valley bottoms, and mountainside clusters of homes. Residents have deep loyalty to their place and a suspicion of other places. There is also a general disdain for urban and industrial ways of life (Halperin 1990).

Contemporary Ethnic Identity

While Appalachian people are culturally similar to many others in rural America, especially the rural South, they retain a special identity connected to the mountains. This identity comes in part from an awareness of the differences between "us and them," an awareness gained most quickly by Appalachians who migrate out of the region and are forced to contend with prejudice and discrimination in cities (Appalshop Films 1983). But these differences are also becoming apparent to Appalachian natives who stay in the mountains, as more and more tourists and newcomers arrive who feel little in common with mountaineers. I moved to western North Carolina almost two decades ago, and my uncle from Idaho came to visit after my daughter was born. I felt sure he would feel comfortable in the mountains since I noticed life was so similar to the rural area in which I was born and raised in the Northwest. But, instead, he was struck by how different the people were in Appalachia, particularly the way they talked, and he couldn't wait to get back home.

The Appalachian dialect is one of the five or six distinctive regional dialects recognized by linguists in the United States (Wolfram and Fasold 1974). In one of the few comprehensive studies of "Appalachian English," Wolfram and Christian (1976) find distinctive phonological and grammatical features, including retaining the initial H in auxiliaries and pronouns ("hit" for "it"), the use of double modal verbs ("I *might could* do that"), and the use of variant pronouns ("hisself" for "himself" and "you'uns" for "all of you"). Social linguists observe that dialect is a primary means by which boundaries of social groups are marked, especially among people otherwise culturally similar. As one of my informants said, "People know who I am the minute I open my mouth." The stigma against "country English" in cities and mainstream America is something that every Appalachian person must contend with in the process of forming a personal identity. By adopting a conscious pride in their cultural heritage, Appalachians are better able to withstand negative images held by others. Some are able actually to exploit the differences, such as best-selling author, Lee Smith, who declares: "The mountains which used to imprison me have become my chosen stalking ground" (Smith 1994).

For Appalachians, there is little consistency in ethnic label identification. The term "Appalachian" is one used by scholars but only rarely assumed by members of the group. More common are identities as "mountain people," "country people," or "mountaineer." Regardless of the lack of agreement on an ethnic name, Appalachian natives can usually identify members of their group through the recognition of an individual's dialect and his or her claims to a homeplace and relatives in the mountains. Appalachians are certainly able to tell you what group they do not belong to, as illustrated in the variety of pejorative names applied to non-Appalachians: Yankee, outsider, "touron" (tourist/moron), "Floron" (Florida resident/moron), and "Floridiot" (Florida resident/idiot). The last three labels derive from gawking and insensitive tourists and seasonal residents who flood the southern mountains for relief from the heat in the summertime. Through careful employment of this oppositional identity, mountaineers tend to continually negotiate their ethnicity, moving in and out of an ethnic group status as they vie for resources and autonomy. Foster (1988) demonstrates this process of shifting ethnicity as native residents of Ashe County, NC, vocally assume a distinctive identity as people with an endangered "mountain culture" in order to stop federal authorities from damming the New River and destroying farmlands. At the same time, residents are not completely comfortable with this identity because of the inferior status conferred on ethnic minority groups in America.

Conclusion

Appalachian ethnicity has emerged out of more than a century of "cultural reflexivity" during which the people have been forced by colonizers and political foes to question their cultural identity and their right to preserve their cultural heritage (Roosens 1989). Their ethnicity has gained strength in an era in which class struggle has become increasingly less successful in organizing in relation to multi-national industries and federal agencies. As ethnics, Appalachians can take advantage of legal precedents and global movements claiming equality and equal treatment for ethnic groups perceived to have the right to retain their culture and define what it consists of (Roosens 1989).

As "reluctant ethnics," Appalachians will continue to negotiate the tensions produced by the inherent contradictions of the core American values of equality (or sameness) and individualism (or differentness) (Hicks & Handler 1988). This tension creates a powerful force in American society especially when these values are consistently at odds with the social reality of ethnic inequality and the power of group labelling. Given their fundamental similarities in race, language, and national origin to white mainstream Americans, mountain people have the option of adopting or resisting ethnic status as it suits their need. As ethnics, they are able to organize, to manipulate symbols of their common heritage, and often to be successful in influencing political policy and the distribution of economic goods. As non-ethnics, they may distance themselves from ascribed ethnic traits, "pass" into the mainstream of American society, and achieve the American Dream in the "melting pot." This strategy of reluctant ethnicity can best be understood as a reasonable Appalachian response to the American context in which individual and group differences are at once denied and celebrated.

References

Richard D. Alba. 1990. *Ethnic Identity: The Transformation of White America.* New Haven: Yale University Press, p. 342.

The Appalachian Regional Commission. 1965. *Appalachia.* Washington, DC: U.S. Government Printing Office.

The Appalachian Land Ownership Task Force. 1983. *Who Owns Appalachia? Landownership and Its Impact.* Lexington, KY: University Press of Kentucky.

Allen Batteau. 1990. *The Invention of Appalachia.* Tucson, AZ: University of Arizona Press.

Patricia D. Beaver. 1986. [reissued 1992]. *Rural Community in the Appalachian South.* Prospect Heights, IL: Waveland Press.

Patricia D. Beaver and Darlene Wilson. March, 1997. "To Embrace the Male Offshore Other: The Ubiquitous Native Grandmother in America's Cultural History," presented at the annual meeting of the Appalachian Studies Association, Fort Mitchell, KY.

Dwight Billings, Kathleen Blee, and Louis Swanson. winter 1986. "Culture, Family, and Community in Preindustrial Apppalachia," *Appalachian Journal*, 13, 154-170.

Ora Blackmun. 1977. *Western North Carolina: Its Mountains and Its People to 1880.* Boone, NC: Appalachian Consortium Press.

H. Tyler Blethen. 1994. "The Transmission of Scottish Culture to the Southern Back Country," in *Appalachian Adaptations to a Changing World*, Journal of the Appalachian Studies Association, ed. Norma Myers, 6, 59-72.

F. Carlene Bryant. 1981. *We're All Kin.* Knoxville, TN: University of Tennessee Press.

Edward J. Cabbell. 1985. "Black Invisibility and Racism in Appalachia: An Informal Survey," in *Blacks in Appalachia*, eds. William H. Turner and Edward J. Cabbell. Lexington: University Press of Kentucky.

John C. Campbell. 1921. *The Southern Highlander & His Homeland.* New York: Russell Sage Foundation, p. 12.

James K. Crissman. 1994. *Death and Dying in Central Appalachia: Changing Attitudes and Practices.* Urbana, IL: University of Illinois Press.

Howard Dorgan. 1987. *Giving Glory to God in Appalachia.* Knoxville, TN: University of Tennessee Press.

Howard Dorgan. 1989. *The Old Regular Baptists of Central Appalachia: Brothers and Sisters in Hope.* Knoxville, TN: University of Tennessee Press.

Ronald D. Eller. 1982. *Miners, Millhands, and Mountaineers: Industrialization of the Appalachian South, 1880-1930.* Knoxville, TN: University of Tennessee Press.

Judith Ivy Fiene. 1993. "The Appalachian Social Context and the Battering of Women," Practicing Anthropology, 15(3) summer, 20-24.

David Hackett Fischer. 1989. *Albion's Seed: Four British Folkways in America.* New York: Oxford University Press.

Thomas R. Ford, ed. 1962. *The Southern Appalachian Region: A Survey.* Lexington, KY: University of Kentucky Press.

Thomas R. Ford. 1962. "The Passing of Provincialism," in *The Southern Appalachian Region: A Survey*, ed. Thomas R. Ford Lexington, KY: University of Kentucky Press.

Stephen William Foster. 1988. *The Past is Another Country: Representation, Historical Consciousness, and Resistance in the Blue Ridge.* Berkeley, CA: University of California Press.

Denise Giardina. 1987. *Storming Heaven: A Novel.* New York: Norton

Rhoda H. Halperin. 1990. *The Livelihood of Kin: Making Ends Meet "The Kentucky Way."* Austin, TX: University of Texas Press.

George L. Hicks. 1976 [reissued 1992]. *Appalachian Valley.* Prospect Heights, IL: Waveland Press.

George L. Hicks and Mark J. Handler. 1987. "Ethnicity, Public Policy, and Anthropologists," in *Applied Anthropology in America*, second edition, eds. Elizabeth M. Eddy and William L. Partridge New York: Columbia University Press.

Charles M. Hudson, ed. 1985. *Ethnology of the Southeastern Indians: A Sourcebook*. New York: Garland Pub.

Richard Humphrey. 1984. presentation at Appalachian State University, Boone, NC.

Richard Humphrey. 1984. "Religion and Place in Southern Appalachia," in *Cultural Adaptations to Mountain Environments*, Southern Anthropological Society Proceedings, No. 17, eds. Patricia D. Beaver and Burton L. Purrington Athens, GA: University of Georgia Press.

John C. Inscoe. 1989. *Mountain Masters: Slavery and the Sectional Crisis in Western North Carolina*. Knoxville, TN: University of Tennessee Press.

Loyal Jones. 1994. *Appalachian Values*. Ashland, KY: The Jesse Stuart Foundation.

Susan E. Keefe. 1985. unpublished field notes.

> 1994. "Urbanism Reconsidered: A Southern Appalachian Perspective," *City and Society*, Annual Review, 1, 20-34.

> 1992. "Reluctant Ethnics: The Interplay of Equality and Individualism in Southern Appalachia," paper presented at the annual meeting of the American Anthropological Association, San Francisco.

> 1988. "Appalachian Family Ties," in *Appalachian Mental Health*, ed. Susan Emley Keefe Lexington, KY: University Press of Kentucky.

Susan E. Keefe and Paul Parsons. March 30, 1996. "A Survey of Appalachian and Non-Appalachian Health and Lifestyles Indicators in Watauga County, NC," presented at the annual meeting of the Appalachian Studies Association, Unicoi, GA.

Susan E. Keefe, Mark D. Vickery, and Karen Dunlap. 1984. "Watauga County Churches," unpublished ms.

Susan E. Keefe, Janice L. Hastrup, and Sherry F. Thomas. November 21, 1993. "Psychological Testing in Rural Appalachia," presented at the annual meeting of the American Anthropological Association, Washington, DC.

Susan E. Keefe, Gregory G. Reck, and Una Mae Lange Reck. 1989. "Measuring Ethnicity and Its Political Consequences in a Southern Appalachian High School," in *Negotiating Ethnicity: The Impact of Anthropological Theory and Practice*, ed. Susan Emley Keefe. Washington, DC: American Anthropological Association, National Association for the Practice of Anthropology, Bulletin No. 8.

Susan E. Keefe, Una Mae Lange Reck, and Gregory G. Reck. 1983. "Ethnicity and Education in Southern Appalachia: A Review," *Ethnic Groups*, 5, 199-226.

Dana Kovarsky, Toby Stephan, and Maria Braswell. 1994. "Conflict Talk in an Appalachian Day Care Center," in *School Discourse Problems*, second edition, eds. Danielle Newberry Ripich and Nancy A. Creaghead San Diego: Singular Publishing.

Helen Matthews Lewis, Linda Johnson, and Donald Askins. 1978. *Colonialism in Modern America: The Appalachian Case*. Boone, NC: Appalachian Consortium Press.

Ronald L. Lewis. 1987. *Black Coal Miners in America: Race, Class, and Community Conflict, 1780-1980*. Lexington, KY: University Press of Kentucky.

Elmora Messer Matthews. 1965. *Neighbor and Kin: Life in a Tennessee Ridge Community*. Nashville, TN: Vanderbilt University Press.

Gordon B. McKinney. 1978. *Southern Mountain Republicans, 1865-1900; Politics and the Appalachian Community*. Chapel Hill, NC: University of North Carolina Press.

Emma Bell Miles. 1975. *The Spirit of the Mountains*. New York: J. Pott, 1905; reprinted Knoxville, TN: University of Tennessee Press.

Teena Morefield. 1990. "The Appalachian Culture: Implications for Counselors," unpublished paper, p. 63.

Robert Morgan. 1987. "Cleaning Off the Cemetary," in *At The Edge of the Orchard Country*. Middletown, CT: Wesleyan University Press, p. 52.

Robert Morgan. 1978. "Mockingbird," in *Trunk and Thicket*. Fort Collins, CO: L'Epervier Press, p. 42.

Sharlotte Neely. 1991. *Snowbird Cherokees: People of Persistence*. Athens, GA: University of Georgia Press.

Gurney Norman. 1972. *Divine Right's Trip*. New York: Dial Press

Marion Pearsall. 1966. "Communicating with the Educationally Deprived," *Mountain Life & Work*, 42(1), 8-11.

William Petersen. 1980. "Concepts of Ethnicity," in *Harvard Encyclopedia of American Ethnic Groups*. Cambridge, MA: Harvard University Press.

Thomas Plaut, Suzanne Landis, and June Trevor. 1993. "Focus Groups and Community Mobilization," in *Successful Focus Groups: Advancing the State of the Art*, ed. David L. Morgan Newbury Park, CA: Sage Press.

Mary Beth Pudup. winter 1990. "The Limits of Subsistence: Agriculture and Industry in Central Appalachia," *Agricultural History*, 64, 61-89.

Karl B. Raitz and Richard Ulack. 1991. "Regional Definitions," in *Appalachia: Social Context Past and Present,* Third edition, eds. Bruce Ergood and Bruce E. Kuhre. Dubuque, IO: Kendall/Hunt.

Eugeen E. Roosens. 1989. *Creating Ethnicity: The Process of Ethnogenesis.* Newbury Park, CA: Sage.

Anya Peterson Royce. 1982. *Ethnic Identity: Strategies of Diversity.* Bloomington, IN: Indiana University Press.

Henry D. Shapiro. 1978. *Appalachia on Our Mind: The Southern Mountains and Mountaineers in the American Consciousness, 1870-1920.* Chapel Hill, NC: University of North Carolina Press, p. x.

Mark Sherrod. 1990. "Asleep in Jesus: Death Rituals in Southern Appalachia," unpublished M.A. thesis, Appalachian State University.

Herb E. Smith. 1983 Strangers & Kin. Whitesburg, KY: Appalshop Films.

Lee Smith. September 8, 1994. "The Terrain of the Heart," convocation address at Appalachian State University, Boone, NC, p.12.

John B. Stephenson. 1968. *Shiloh: A Mountain Community.* Lexington, KY: University of Kentucky Press.

John B. Stephenson and L. Sue Greer. 1983. "Ethnographers in Their Own Cultures: Two Appalachian Cases," *Human Organization*, 40, 123-130.

James Still. 1986. "Heritage," in *The Wolfpen Poems*. Frankfort, KY: Berea College Press, distributed by Gnomon Distribution, p. 82.

    1940 *River of Earth*. New York: The Viking Press.

Ivan Tribe. 1991. "Traditional Appalachian Music/Early Commercial Country Music: Continuity and Transition," in *Appalachia: Social Context Past and Present*, Third edition, eds. Bruce Ergood and Bruce E. Kuhre. Dubuque, IO: Kendall/Hunt.

William H. Turner. 1985. "The Demography of Black Appalachia: Past and Present," in *Blacks in Appalachia,* eds. William H. Turner and Edward J. Cabbell, Lexington, KY: University Press of Kentucky, p. 257.

William H. Turner. 1985. "Introduction," in *Blacks in Appalachia*, eds. William H. Turner and Edward J. Cabbell, Lexington, KY: University Press of Kentucky, p. xix.

US Bureau of the Census. 1992. *1990 Census of Population, Supplementary Reports, Detailed Ancestry Groups for States,* Washington, DC: US Government Printing Office.

US Bureau of the Census. *1990 Census of Population, Supplementary Reports, Detailed Ancestry Groups for States.*

Melinda Bollar Wagner, Shannon T. Scott, Megan Scanlon, Stacy L. Viers, and Jean A. Kappes. 1995. "It May Not Be Heaven, But It's Close:" Land and People in Craig County, Virginia," Radford, VA: Radford University Appalachian Regional Study Center.

Altina L. Waller. 1988. *Feud: Hatfields, McCoys, and Social Change in Appalachia, 1860-1900.* Chapel Hill, NC: University of North Carolina Press.

David Walls. 1978. "Internal Colony or Internal Periphery? A Critique of Current Models and an Alternative Formulation," in *Colonialism in Modern America: The Appalachian Case,* eds. Helen Matthews Lewis, Linda Johnson, and Donald Askins Boone, NC: Appalachian Consortium Press.

Mary Waters. 1990. *Ethnic Options.* Berkeley: University of California Press.

Jack E. Weller. 1965. *Yesterday's People: Life in Contemporary Appalachia.* Lexington, KY: University of Kentucky Press.

David E. Whisnant. 1983. *All That is Native & Fine*. Chapel Hill, NC: University of North Carolina Press.

Eliot Wigginton and Margie Bennett, eds. 1984. *Foxfire 8.* New York: 1st Anchor Books.

Charles Williams. 1982. "The Conversion Ritual in a Rural Black Baptist Church," in *Holding on to the Land and the Lord: Kinship, Ritual, Land Tenure, and Social Policy in the Rural South*, Southern Anthropological Society Proceedings, No. 15, eds. Robert L. Hall and Carol B. Stack Athens, GA: University of Georgia Press.

J.W. Williamson. 1995. *Hillbillyland: What the Movies Did to the Mountains and What the Mountains Did to the Movies.* Chapel Hill, NC: University of North Carolina Press.

Margaret R. Wolfe. 1980-81. "The Appalachian Reality: Ethnic and Class Diversity,' *East Tennessee Historical Society's Publications*, 52, 40-60.

Walt Wolfram and Donna Christian. 1976. *Appalachian Speech.* Arlington, VA: Center for Applied Linguistics.

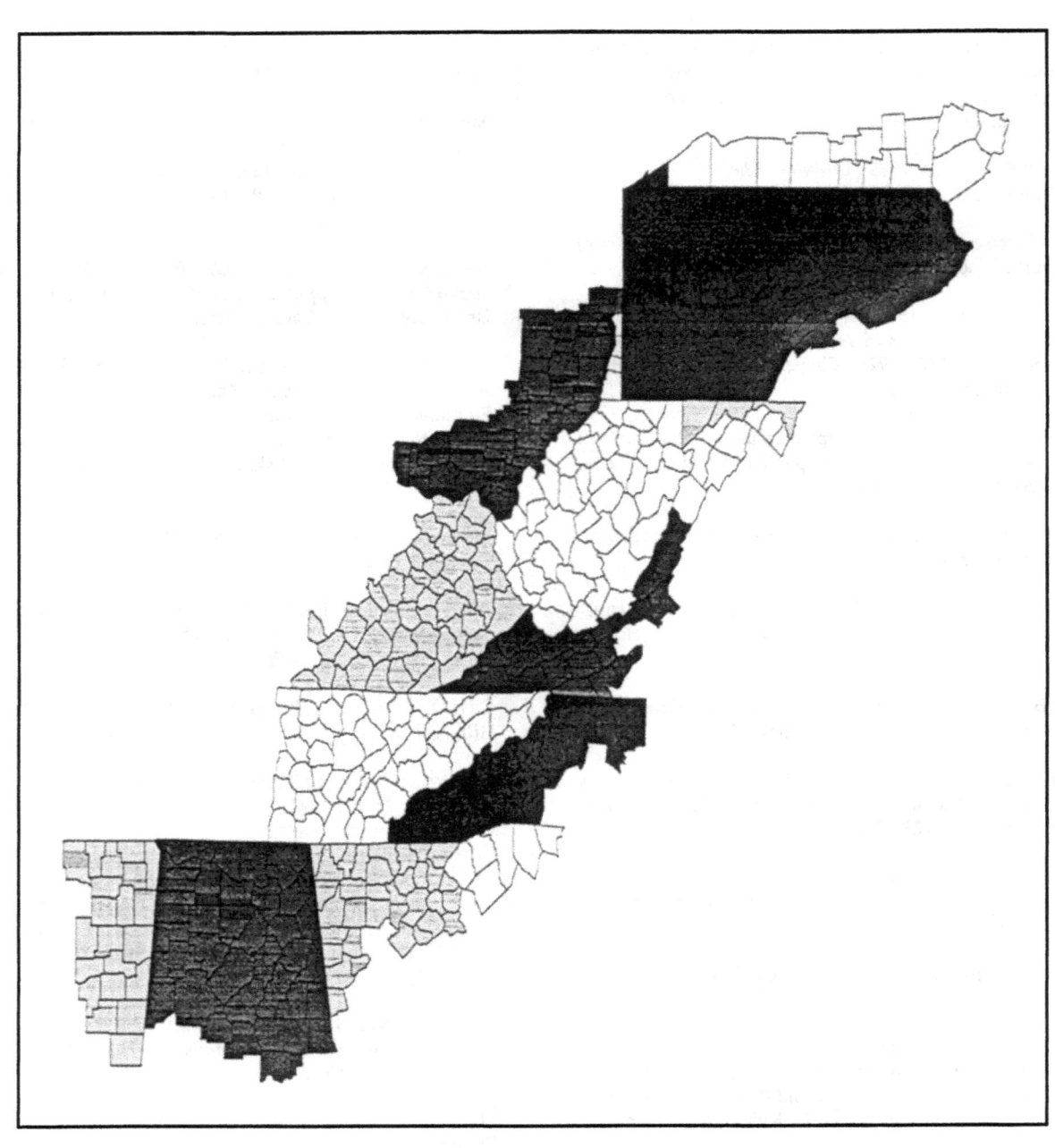

Appalachia as defined by the Appalachian Regional Commission in 1996: 399 counties in 13 states

II. Exploring a Region through Quantitative Data

Frequencies and Percentages

Welcome to Appalachia and the world of social research. You have new technology at your fingertips to explore the region's geography, settlement patterns, successes and problems. You will be using a "student version" of the MicroCase statistics package with real data gathered from a variety of government and private agency sources.

The MicroCase software enables you to conduct professional analyses and yet it is easy to use-- you'll master its basic commands in a few minutes. By the end of this workbook, you should have a good understanding of the Appalachian Region, be able to conduct your own research, have a solid introduction to the uses of quantitative statistics and be comfortable using computers for research and data analysis.

GETTING STARTED

The MicroCase statistics software requires an IBM-PC or fully compatible computer with 640K of memory (RAM) and a VGA graphics card.

To use the MicroCase program the first time, it's helpful to pair up with a friend or fellow student. One of you can operate the computer while the other reads the instructions. After the first few minutes, you'll be comfortable enough with the program to work individually.

To begin, place the disk in the 3.5 inch floppy drive--the A or B drive. Your computer monitor should be displaying the "C prompt," which looks like "C:>". *Type* **A:** (or **B:** if the disk is in the B drive) and *press* *<ENTER>*. The computer will change the prompt from the C drive to the A or B drive. When you see A: (or B:) *type* **MC** and *press* *<ENTER>*. (If you run the program from a Windows environment, you may need to *type* **MCIII** and *press* *<ENTER>*.)

Once you have typed MC and *pressed* *<ENTER>*, it will take about 30 seconds for the program to load. The first time you start Student MicroCase, you will be asked to enter your name. It is important to type your name correctly, since it will appear on all printed output. Type in your name and *press* *<ENTER>*. If it is correct, simply *press* *<ENTER>* in response to the next prompt. (If you need to make a correction, *type* **Y** at the prompt and *press* *<ENTER>*. The copyright screen will appear. *Press* *<ENTER>* to continue to the first of two primary menus. Its border will be blue and labeled **DATA AND FILE MANAGEMENT**. The menu shows all the choices available with the complete MicroCase statistics package (A through P). The choices you are allowed to make with this abbreviated "student version" of the MicroCase Analysis System are in a darker print and starred, for example

> ***I. Open, Look, Erase or Copy File.** This is the place to start and you will see that it is automatically marked with a box. (You can move the box with the arrow keys.)

The menu looks like this:

```
                    DATA AND FILE MANAGEMENT

*S. Switch to STATISTICAL ANALYSIS MENU

DATA MANAGEMENT
        A. Define Variables/Recodes          *E. Codebook
        B. Collapse/Strip Categories          F. Edit Variable Information
        C. Enter Data from Keyboard           G. Grading Recode
        D. List or Print Variable Values      H. Setup Data Entry

FILE MANAGEMENT
        *I. Open, Look, Erase or Copy File    M. Move Data between Files
        J. Create New Data File               N. Merge Files
        K. Create Subset File                 O. Create Aggregation File
        L. Import/Export Data                 P. Create Statistical Summary

*X. EXIT from MicroCase

                                              OPEN FILE:C:\APCOUNTY
```

Note that **I. Open, Look, Erase or Copy File** is highlighted by a box around it. *Press <ENTER>* and you will see a single file: **APCOUNTY**. *Press <ENTER>* again and you will see a new screen with "File Name:C:\APCOUNTY" at the top. Below is a description of the file: "Data on the 399 Federally-designated Appalachian Counties" and a list including the Current Number of Cases: 399. Each of the federally designated Appalachian Region's 399 counties is a case. (The county is the *unit of analysis* in this data base; other studies might use census tracts, states or nations as the unit of analysis. Surveys use individuals as the unit of analysis.) Next you will see the number of variables: 90. You will be able to compare each of the 399 counties across these 90 variables. For example, you can compare counties in terms of how much money people make (per capita income), average levels of education, percentage of the labor force engaged in mining, percentage of voters who favored Clinton in 1990, etc. *Press <ENTER>* to continue. Note that the functions that can be used with this trimmed-down version of the software are starred (*). You need the full MicroCase Analysis System to access all the functions. *Press* the **S. Switch to STATISTICAL ANALYSIS** menu function (which should have the highlighting box around it) to obtain a listing of statistical procedures. The STATISTICAL ANALYSIS menu has a red border to clearly differentiate it from the blue-bordered DATA FILE AND MANAGEMENT menu. You move between the two menus by *pressing* **S**. The STATISTICAL ANALYSIS menu looks like this:

```
                    STATISTICAL ANALYSIS

    *S. Switch to DATA AND FILE MANAGEMENT MENU

    DATA MANAGEMENT
            *A. Univariate Statistics          *F. Scatterplot
            *B. Tabular Statistics             *G. Correlation
            *C. Analysis of Variance           H. Partial Correlation
            D. Covariance Analysis             *I. Regression
            *E. Mapping Variables

    ADVANCED STATISTICAL ANALYSIS
            J. Regession Models                L. Factor Analysis
            K. Curve Fitting                   M. Logistic Regression
                                               N. Time Series

    Q. Interactive Batch

    *X. EXIT from MicroCase

                                               OPEN FILE:C:\APCOUNTY
```

OK. You're ready to start exploring Appalachia. *Press* **E. Mapping Variables**. At the prompt "Enter name or number of variable to be mapped:" *type* **2** and *press* *<ENTER>*. A map of the Appalachian region will unfold across the screen, state by state. Colors will be added and you will be able to see Appalachia's 399 counties spread across portions of 12 states and all of West Virginia. The Federal Government has determined that Appalachia consists of 399 counties in 13 states. *Press* **D** (for distribution) and you will see a list of the counties and states. (Don't worry about the numbers to the right of the county names--I used them here only to color code the states so they would stand out from each other on the map.) *Press the Page Down key* to scroll down the 399 counties and *make a list* of Appalachia's thirteen states:

1 _____   8 _____

2 _____   9 _____

3 _____   10 _____

4 _____   11 _____

5 _____   12 _____

6 _____   13 _____

7 _____

Press <ENTER> to return to the map and *press* <ENTER> again to get the variable prompt. *Type 3 and press <ENTER>*. You will see Appalachia divided into three regions: Northern, Central and Southern. In 1974, Appalachian Regional Commission (ARC) planners decided these regions have different strengths and needs that required different strategies for development:

> The Northern region (coded yellow) includes portions of New York, Pennsylvania, Ohio, Maryland and all but the nine most southeastern counties of West Virginia. Seen as an area having an old or outmoded manufacturing economic base, the 1990 per capita income was $17,265 or 83.6% of the U.S. average, $20,652.

> The Central Appalachian region (orange) contains the bituminous coal fields and timber. The ARC said that the region had been "plagued for decades" with socio-economic deficiencies. 1990 per capita income was only $13,073 (76% of the Northern Appalachian subregion and 63.3 % of the U.S. average). Why should an area so rich in resources be so poor? The commission cited the rough mountain terrain and an economy focused on the coal industry (*Appalachia* magazine, Vol. 8, No. 1, August-September 1974, pp. 10-27). Some critics, such as Jack Weller in his book *Yesterday's People,* saw problems in the values and world views of mountain people, while others, such as Helen Lewis (see "Fatalism or the Coal Industry" in Ergood and Kuhre's *Appalachia; Social context, Past, Present and Future)* traced the problem to damage done by extractive (coal and timber) industries and corporations and government policy. Were the region's problems caused by the values of its residents, or by historical events, such as industrialization? The data you will explore in the coming chapters should help you formulate your own opinion.

> The Southern region (red), running from the Blue Ridge of Virginia to Mississippi, was described by ARC planners as an area "moving from an agrarian-based economy to a new, modern industrial economy with rapid population growth being the outstanding characteristic of the region." The ARC called for balanced growth between urban and rural areas, diversification of employment opportunities, and a new leadership for economic development. Its 1990 per capita income was $16,893 or 81.8% of the U.S. average.

Let's see how many counties are in each of the three regions. *Press <ENTER>* until you return to the **STATISTICAL ANALYSIS** menu. *Select* **A. Univariate Statistics.** At the "Enter the name or number of the variable" prompt, *type* **3** *and press <ENTER>*. Bypass the next request for a subset variable by *pressing <ENTER>* and you will see a "pie chart" containing three slices, each representing one of the three regions. *Press the up or down arrow key* and you will see a slice "exploded" away from the rest of the pie and identified as "North 144 36.1%," "Central 84 21.1%" or "Southern 171 42.9%." Translated, this means the Northern subregion as having 144 counties, or 36.1 percent of the total of Appalachia's 399 counties. The Central subregion has 84 counties or 21 percent and the Southern has 171 counties or 42.9 percent. *Press* **T** and you will see a table. Fill in the blanks (ignoring the columns listing cumulative percent (Cum.%) and Z-Score):

Table 1: Number of Counties in the Appalachian Sub-Regions

	Frequency	%
North		
Central		
Southern		

Tables such as this one usually add another row for totals and look like this:

Table 1a: Number of Counties in the Appalachian Sub-Regions

	Frequency	%
North		
Central		
Southern		
Total	399	100

Press <ENTER> twice to return to the **STATISTICAL ANALYSIS** menu and *select* **E. Mapping Variables.** *Press the* **F3** *function key at the top of your keyboard.* A list of all 90 variables in the **APCOUNTY** data file will appear. You can use the *arrow* keys to scroll down the list, the *page down/up* keys to jump down a full screen of 17 variables and the *home* and *end* keys to move to the beginning and the end of the list. You can either enter a variable's number at the prompt (as you have already done in previous exercises), or you can use the *left arrow* key to mark a variable. Practice this by *pressing* **F3** *to obtain the list of 90 variables. Arrow down* to 5) Highlands on the F3 variable list and *press the left arrow to mark it. Press <ENTER>* to see a map of those counties designated as "highlands" by ARC planners, who defined them as areas over 1,000 feet above sea level, which consequently have good potential for recreational development. *Press* **F3** again to see that you can obtain the variables list as an overlay on the map.

Okay, let's see if you can repeat the process you did for the three Appalachian subregions and create a table showing highland and non-highland counties. *Press <ENTER> three times* to return to the **STATISTICAL ANALYSIS** menu. *Press* **A. Univariate Statistics.** At the variable prompt, *press* **F3**, *arrow down* to 5)Highlands, *press the left arrow to mark it and press <ENTER> twice* to bypass the request for a subset. (Don't worry about subsets now; they will be explained in chapter 5.) The pie chart should look like an environmentally (politically?) correct scene, portraying a blue sky above a slightly tilted green mountain. Matching the color code legend in the upper left of the monitor screen with the pie chart, you can see that a majority of Appalachian counties are not highland counties. *Press* **T** (for Table) and fill in the following blanks:

Table 2. Highland and Non-Highland Appalachian Counties

	Frequency	%
Not High		
Highlands		
Total		

Well done! In these first few pages you have learned how to define Appalachia and its three subregions. You've learned how to access the MicroCase software package, open a data file, make maps and simple tables to describe *univariate* (one variable) data. In future chapters, you will learn how to compare two variables (*bivariate* data) or several variables (*multivariate* data). Simple practice will enable you to move about the MicroCase software comfortably. Practice--*playing with data*--is central to learning the basic elements of data analysis and how to use the software. *The more you play, the more you'll know.* It's similar to learning how to ride a bike or drive a car.

At this point I need to explain that statistical maps are not usually used to block out subregions of an area. It's been a good way to introduce you to the software and to Appalachia, but the mapping function is really used to portray the *distribution* of variables: For example, where is unemployment the highest (and the lowest)? *Press <ENTER> twice* to return to the **STATISTICAL ANALYSIS** menu and *select* **E. Mapping Variables.** *Press* **F3** and *type* **S**. At the *Phrase* prompt, *type* "unemployment" and *press <ENTER>*. A second box appears, listing two variables related to unemployment: 37)UNEMP91 and 38)UNEMP80. Use the left arrow to *mark* 37)UNEMP91 and *press <ENTER> twice* to obtain a map of 1991 CIVILIAN LABOR FORCE UNEMPLOYMENT.

Take a tour of the black prompts bar at the bottom of the screen. **Dist.** stands for *distribution* of cases, from the highest rate or percentage to the lowest. (You used this function previously to discover the states with counties in Appalachia, but, technically, it was not a correct use of the function because there was no rank ordering of states from high to low--it was just a simple list.) If you *press* **D**, you will find that Graham County, North Carolina has the highest unemployment rate (25.7%), followed by Elliott County, Kentucky (22.6%). The screen displays the highest 50 cases. Since there are 399 cases over all, you would have to press the Page Down function key seven times to find the county with the lowest unemployment rate, which is Tompkins County, NY (3.4 percent). *Press* **A** (for area) to return to the map and *press* **L** for the map's legend, showing the color-coded breakdown of the distribution into five clusters, ranked from lowest to highest scores. *Press <ENTER>* to return to the map and *press* **S** for spot, which recreates the map with spots and colors depicting unemployment rates. Messy, isn't it? With so many cases (399), spot maps aren't very helpful. **Comp** allows the comparison of maps for two variables; we will do this in the next chapter. **Name** points to the county with the highest rate; you can move down the list by using the down arrow key. "Print" enables the printing of maps.

For practice, use the F3 key and the mapping and distribution functions to discover which

    of the three regions is the most rural   _____

    of the three regions has the most mining   _____

    county has the highest mean per capita income   _____

    county has the highest level of education   _____

    county has most doctors per person   _____

Which Appalachian county is the most interesting to you? Why?

_____

_____

Welcome to Appalachia, and a computerized statistical package that enables exploration of a region similar in many ways to the nation that surrounds it, while also maintaining its own unique characteristics.

Throughout this book, you will be asked to translate data into your own words. Describing data is a skill that requires practice to learn. Begin this learning process now by writing summary statements about

    Appalachia and its constituent states and number of counties

    Appalachia's three regions and their differences

The computer maps and what they can demonstrate.

What **frequencies** can tell you.

Why **percentages** are more helpful in explaining data than frequencies.

Some students enjoy summarizing data with computer slide presentation software, such as Microsoft's PowerPoint or Corel's Presentations. You may want to experiment with one of these programs as a means of presenting and explaining data.

Appalachian Settlement Patterns:
Discovering a Multi-Cultural Region

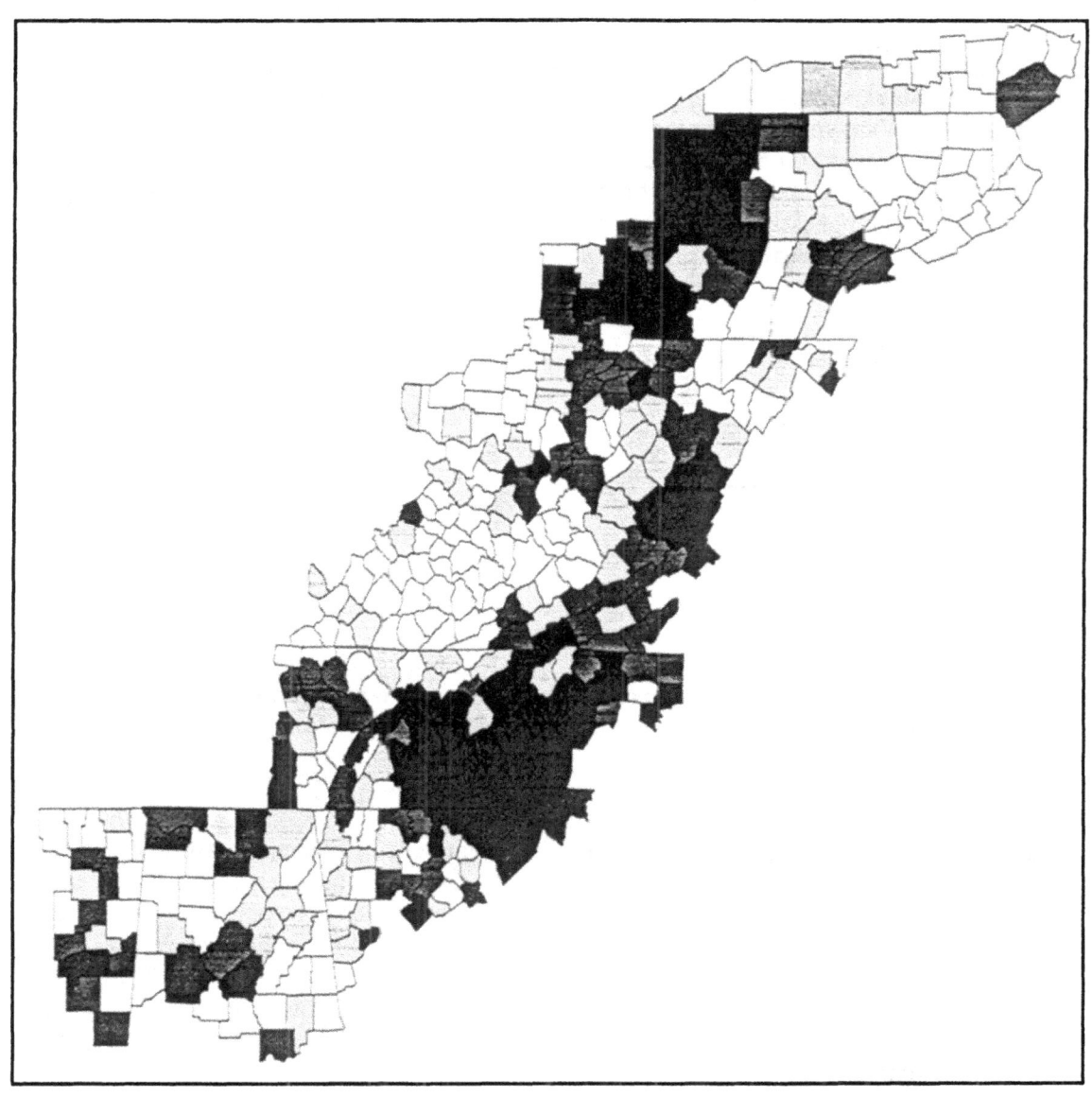

1990 Census: Percent claiming Scotch-Irish Ancestry

III. Cultural Diversity in Appalachia

Mapping, Rank Ordering and Correlation Coefficients

Appalachia enjoys a rich multi-cultural diversity. There are Native Americans and African Americans, Scotch-Irish, German and Italians. Ever heard of the Pennsylvania Dutch? They're not Dutch. They're *Deutsche*--German. Let's see where the Germans settled in Appalachia.

Open the **APCOUNTY** file, switch to the red **STATISTICAL ANALYSIS MENU**. Place the highlight on **E. Mapping Variables** and press *<Enter>*. Now the screen asks you for the variable you want to map. Type **13** or **%German90**. What you are mapping is the percent of people in a county who reported any German ancestry in the 1990 census. *Type* **N** (for Name) to see which county has the highest percentage of people claiming German ancestry. Snyder, Pa. has the highest percentage: 66.07%. *Press the down arrow* to find the county with the next highest rate. It is Holmes, Ohio, with a rate of 64.86%. *Press <ENTER>* to return to the map and *press* **D** (for distribution). You will see a list of all 399 counties, listed from the county with the highest percent to the lowest. Snyder, Pa. should be at the top. List the top five counties:

1. Snyder, Pa. _____

2. _____

3. _____

4. _____

5. _____

Press the DOWN ARROW repeatedly (seven times) to scroll down to the bottom of the list of 399 counties. You will find that Benton County, Mississippi has the fewest people claiming German ancestry. List the percentage of people claiming German ancestry in Benton County: _____.

Notice that there is a *color coding* of the county names. The entire list is broken into fifths, each with its own color. *Press <ENTER>* to return to the map and *type* **L** (for Legend). The legend indicates the ranges used for clustering the counties into five groups (quintiles) of 80 counties each (except for the lowest group which has 79--with 399 counties, one of the clusters had to get short changed.) The highest quintile has counties with percentages of persons claiming German ancestry ranging from 32.90 to 66.87 percent. The lowest quintile has percentages of persons claiming German ancestry ranging from 3.36 to 10.28 percent. *Press <ENTER>* and look at the map again. Notice how the color coding provides you a quick, graphic view of where Germans settled in Appalachia.

The Scotch-Irish also settled in Appalachia. Return to the red **STATISTICAL ANALYSIS MENU**. Place the highlight on **E. Mapping Variables** and press *<Enter>*. Type **15** or **%SCT.IRH90.** Do you see any clusters of Scotch-Irish? *Press* **D** (for distribution) and list the ten counties where the highest percentage of people claim Scotch-Irish ancestry:

1. _____

2. _____

3. _____

4. _____

5. _____

6. _____

7. _____

8. _____

9. _____

10. _____

In which <u>state</u> did the most people claim Scotch-Irish heritage? _____

Who are the Scotch-Irish? What can you learn about their origins and the routes they traveled into the mountains? One good source is John C. Campbell's chapter on "Pioneer Routes of Travel and Early Settlements" in his classic <u>The Southern Highlander and His Homeland</u>. (His chapter is reprinted in the Ergood and Kurhre reader cited in the Resources listing on page 113).

_____

_____

_____

_____

_____

_____

_____

_____

_____

What does Susan Emley Keefe say in Chapter 1 about the ethnic identity of the Scotch-Irish, and why might there may be a significant undercount in the numbers of Scotch-Irish claiming their heritage in the 1990 census?

_____

_____

_____

_____

_____

_____

_____

_____

The first inhabitants of Appalachia were Native Americans. They arrived in Appalachia long before the Germans, Scotch-Irish and other Europeans and they still thrive in the mountains today. Can you find the counties and states where descendants of Native Americans are clustered? Return to the **STATISTICAL ANALYSIS** menu. Place the highlight on **E. Mapping Variables** and press *<Enter>*. *Type* **11** or **%AMER.IN90**. Do you see any clusters of Native Americans? *Press* **D** (for distribution) and list the five counties where the highest percentage of people claim such ancestry:

1. _____

2. _____

3. _____

4. _____

5. _____

What state is most represented? _____

Does this state rank high in terms of people claiming German ancestry?   Yes   No

Does this state rank high in terms of people claiming Scotch-Irish ancestry?   Yes   No

Do you know what tribe is represented in the high ranked counties? It's the Cherokee. Any web browser such as http://www.google.com/ will take you to web sites containing information on Cherokee history and culture. Record below what you can find out about famous Cherokee leaders and important dates in the history of the Cherokee people. One good web site is http://www.tolatsga.org/Cherokee1.html and http://www.tolatsga.org/Cherokee2.html (This site also has a Cherokee2.html.)

_____

_____

_____

_____

_____

_____

_____

_____

Ever hear of the Trail of Tears? Read an eyewitness account by a soldier on the march at http://www.powersource.com/cherokee/burnett.html. What did you learn from John G. Burnett's account of the removal of the Cherokees from Western North Carolina?

_____

_____

_____

_____

_____

_____

_____

_____

Few people realize that African Americans have a proud history in Appalachia. They built the railroads and many worked in the coal mines. Return to the **STATISTICAL ANALYSIS** menu. Place the highlight on **E. Mapping Variables** and press *<Enter>*. *Type* **18** or **%BLACK90**. Where is the black population? **D** (for distribution) and list the five counties where the highest percentage of people claim African American ancestry:

1. _____

2. _____

3. _____

4. _____

5. _____

What state is most represented? _____

Are Blacks and Germans clustered in the same parts of Appalachia?   Yes   No

Clearly the states having the highest African-American population are in the Deep South, where the plantation economy was driven by the engine of slave and tenant farmer labor. But Blacks also joined the migration north to the coal fields. *Type* **N** (for Name) and use the *down arrow* to find the counties in West Virginia, Pennsylvania and Ohio ranked with the highest percentage of Black population. List them:

1. _____

2. _____

3. _____

4. _____

5. _____

6. _____

7. _____

8. _____

Did people of different nationalities cluster together in Appalachia? Return to the **STATISTICAL ANALYSIS** menu. Place the highlight on **E. Mapping Variables** and press <*Enter*>. Now *press F3* and you will see a list of all the variables in the APCOUNTY data file. Note that variables 11-13 all deal with the percentage of people claiming different ethnic or national ancestry. *Type 12* or **%ENGLISH90** and *press <ENTER>* to find what portion of Appalachia has the most people claiming English ancestry. Look at the map carefully and note where the English settled. *Press* **C** (for comparison) and, when you are asked for the **Name or number of variable for comparison**, *type* **16 or %SCOTTSH90**.

Do the two maps look the same?   Yes   No

Does it appear that the English and the Scottish settled in the same area?   Yes   No

In the top right-hand corner of the screen is the equation r = _____. (Enter the number.)

The letter "r" stands for the **Pearson Product-Moment correlation coefficient.** It is a measure of the *strength* and *direction* of a relationship between two variables (such as %ENGLISH90 and %SCOTTISH90).

The direction may be *positive* (the more of one, the more of the other), or *negative* (the more of one, the less of the other).

Relationships between variables also differ in terms of *strength*. The closer r is to 1 (+1 or -1), the stronger the association. William Fox suggests the following "rough" guide to strength of association:

  Scores above 0.70 suggest a *very strong* association between two variables.
  Scores between 0.50 and 0.70 indicate a *strong* association.
  Scores in the 0.20-0.50 range are considered *moderate*.
  Scores between 0.10-0.20 *are weak* and
  Scores less than 0.10 suggest virtually no relationship between variables.

Put another way, if the compared maps were identical, r would equal 1. (If you compared 13)%GERMAN WITH 13)%GERMAN, r = 1.) When the maps indicate people live in different areas, there is a negative r: for 13)%GERMAN90 and 18)%BLACK90 is -0.351, indicating a *moderate, negative association* (where there are more Germans, there are less African Americans). If r is close to 0, (for 12)%ENGLISH and 11)%AMER.IN90 r=0.004), there is no relationship between the two variables.

Press <ENTER> to clear the lower map and, at the prompt for a new comparison variable, *type* **15** or **%SCT.IRH90**.

Do the two maps look the same?   Yes   No

Does it appear that the English and the Scotch-Irish settled in the same area?   Yes   No

     r = _____

Press <ENTER> to clear the lower map and, at the prompt for a new comparison variable, *type* **11** or **%AMER.IND90**.

Do the two maps look the same?   Yes   No

Does it appear that the English and Native Americans settled in the same area?   Yes   No

     r = _____

Use "F3" function key to find the variables needed to determine the correlations between people claiming

    English and Scottish ancestry   0.63

    English and Scotch-Irish ancestry   _____

    English and Native American ancestry   _____

    German and Italian ancestry   _____

    German and Black ancestry   _____

    German and Native American ancestry   _____

Would you say that...

    English and Scottish people seem to have settled in the same areas?

                     Yes   Not really   Clearly not   (circle one)

    There is a strong   moderate - weak - nonexistent (circle one) correlation
    between these two variables.

English and Scotch-Irish people seem to have settled in the same areas?

            Yes Not really Clearly not

 There is a strong moderate - weak - nonexistent (circle one) correlation between these two variables.

English and Native American people seem to have settled in the same areas?

            Yes Not really Clearly not

 There is a strong moderate - weak - nonexistent (circle one) correlation between these two variables

German and Italian people seem to have settled in the same areas?

            Yes Not really Clearly not (circle one)

 There is a strong moderate - weak - nonexistent (circle one) correlation between these two variables.

German and Black Americans seem to have settled in the same areas?

            Yes Not really Clearly not

 There is a strong moderate - weak - nonexistent (circle one) correlation between these two variables.

German and Native American people seem to have settled in the same areas?

            Yes Not really Clearly not

 There is a strong moderate - weak - nonexistent (circle one) correlation between these two variables.

Now use the codebook function to determine the mean (average) percentage of people in various states claiming different kinds of ethnic heritage. *Press <ENTER>* until you return to the STATISTICAL ANALYSIS menu. *Press* **S** to switch to the blue DATA AND FILE MANAGEMENT menu. *Select* **E. Codebook** and follow these instructions carefully:

> When asked to "Select output device," *type* **1** and *press <ENTER>* (to send the data to the screen). *Type* **Y**, when asked if you want to stratify (which in this case means break the data down by the thirteen states having counties in Appalachia). *Enter* **89)**STATESCODE as the stratifying variable. *Press <ENTER>* to accept 89)STATESCODE as the independent variable. *Press <ENTER>* again to bypass the request for a subset.
>
> When asked for a "list of variables to be included," *type* **12,13,15,18** and *press <ENTER>*.

You should see the first of four tables, which list "N" counties by each of the 13 states, together with their mean (average) percentage of people claiming English ancestry. The state claiming the highest English ancestry is _____.

Take a moment to list the number of Appalachian counties in each state:

New York	_____
Pennsylvania	_____
Maryland	_____
Ohio	_____
West Virginia	_____
Virginia	_____
Kentucky	_____
Tennessee	_____
North Carolina	_____
South Carolina	_____
Georgia	_____
Alabama	_____
Mississippi	_____

Total Appalachian Counties _____

> *Press <ENTER>* to find the <u>two</u> states with the highest mean claims to <u>German</u> ancestry. Those states are _____ and _____.

> *Press <ENTER>* to find the two states with the highest average citations of <u>Scotch-Irish</u> ancestry. They are _____ and _____.

> *Press <ENTER>* to find the single state where people claim the highest <u>African-American</u> ancestry, which is _____.

To summarize this chapter, you have learned

> that Appalachia is not a homogeneous stronghold of Anglo-Saxon stock, but rather a heterogeneous, multi-cultural region.
>
> that different groups settled in different parts of the region: Germans in Pennsylvania and Maryland, the Scotch-Irish in the Carolinas, etc.
>
> that some ethnic groups tended to settle near each other.
>
> how to make and read MicroCase maps and how to compare maps.
>
> how to find distributions of cases.
>
> how to interpret the *correlation coefficient* "r" as a measure of both the strength and direction of an association between two variables.
>
> how to use the *codebook* function to review data and break data down by units such as states (or regions, etc.).

Make a presentation describing settlement patterns and ethnic diversity in the Appalachian region. If available, use computer software such as Microsoft's PowerPoint or Corel's Presentations. If such programs are not available, you can use newsprint and markers. As previously noted, John C. Campbell's chapter on "Pioneer Routes of Travel and Early Settlements" in The Southern Highlander and His Homeland is an excellent resource, as is Susan Emley Keefe's introduction to the region in Chapter 1.

IV. Demographics: Urbanization and Migration in Appalachia

Mapping and Regression

Demographics is the study of population and population movements. It looks for characteristics of size, density and migrations of human populations. Now that you know something of the ethnic diversity of the region, look for the concentrations of populations. *Open the APCOUNTY file and select* **A. Univariate statistics**. At the prompt, *type* **6** and *press <ENTER> twice,* bypassing the request for a subset. You will see a "pie chart" indicating the ratio of metro to nonmetro counties. About a quarter of the pie is metro--25 percent. *Press the down arrow key* to "explode" the pie, emphasizing the metro piece. This is a simple way of making a chart a little more dramatic for presentation. *Press T* to obtain a table which indicates that 75.4 percent of the 399 Appalachian counties (N=301) are nonmetro. Some 24.6 counties (N=98) are metro.

> **Univariate statistics** are best employed with *"categorical"* variables such as City (NONMETRO=0, METRO=1), or Three Region (North=1, Central=2, Southern=3). Categorical variables usually have less than 10 *values* (scores). *"Interval/ratio"* variables are numbers, rates or percentages (1,2,3,4,5....100) and thus can have hundreds of values. If you use interval/ratio variables in a pie chart, you have "too many pieces" of pie. MicroCase will provide a pie chart or bar chart for categorical variables such as 3)Three Regn and 6)City, but not for continuous variables like 7 (%URBAN). To get around this problem, researchers "collapse" continuous variables into categorical ones (1-20=category 1; 21-39=2, etc.) and end up with 2 - 10 readily understandable/consumable/digestible slices of data. Variable 85 (%URB90COL) is the *continuous* variable 7 (%URBAN) collapsed into five categories.

Select **E. Mapping Variables**. At the prompt, *type* **6** and *press <ENTER>*. You will see a two color map indicating counties in (or not in) metropolitan areas variously called "MSAs" for Metropolitan Statistical Areas or variations on the same name, such as CMSA=Consolidated Metropolitan Statistical Area. Definitions vary from census to census, but, in general terms, a **metropolitan area** consists of a central city area of at least 50,000 people, together with any surrounding counties tied to the city by economic and commuting patterns for work and services. If you compare the map you see on your monitor to an atlas, you will find the clusters of counties that make up the metropolitan areas around Birmingham, Ala; Atlanta, Ga; Greenville, SC; Roanoke, VA.; the Knoxville-Bristol corridor in Tennessee; Charleston, W.Va., and Pittsburgh (and much of industrial Pennsylvania). Metropolitan areas appear throughout the mountain region.

Press **Comp**. The screen will divide in two and take about 20 seconds to make a smaller map of the Appalachian region. You will be asked for the "Name or number of variable for comparison:" *Enter* **7**. Another map will appear showing the counties by percentage of population living in urban areas (places of 2,500 people or more). The counties with the highest urban population should be among the counties listed as "MSA, etc." counties in the top map. Let's see if this works: *Press <ENTER>* three times to return to the variable prompt and *type* **7**. After the map appears *press* **D** and write down the 10 counties with the highest percentage of population living in urban areas:

Allegheny, PA. 95.9%   _____

_____   _____

_____   _____

_____   _____

_____   _____

Press <ENTER> three times to return to the variable prompt and *type* **6** to recover the Metro map and *type* **D** (for distribution). You'll see 50 counties listed, all coded as "1," meaning they are "metro" counties. *Press the down arrow* to go to the second screen. You'll see another 48 counties listed as metro and the last two as non-metro (coded as "0"). (If you continued to down arrow through the rest of the counties, you would find them all coded as non metro.) *Press the home key* to return to the top of the distribution list. You should find all of the counties listed above in the metro counties.

Another way to look at population is in terms of density, measured as the number of people per square mile. It stands to reason that the highest population density should be in urban areas. Compare variable 7 (1990: PERCENT URBAN) to variable 84 (1990: PERCENT PER SQUARE MILE). Do the maps look the same?

_____yes   _____no, not really

Look at the correlation coefficient r in the upper right hand corner of the screen. (To review what "r" is and how it works refer back to page 16 in Chapter 2.)

The correlation r is _____. It is   weak   moderate   strong   (circle one).

Look at the maps closely and describe the areas where population density is the highest.

_____

_____

_____

_____

_____

Migration patterns can tell a lot about an area. People like to move and stay in places where there are good jobs, schools and services--in sum, where there is a good quality of life. When an economy weakens and jobs disappear, people move elsewhere in search of a better life. In the 1940s and 50s, more than three million people left Appalachia for work in northern and Midwestern cities. In the 1980s, some parts of the Appalachian region lost population while other parts gained it. The MicroCase **mapping** function shows what areas of the region lost and gained populations. The **scatterplot** function provides data on associations between migration and levels of income, poverty, etc.

Select **E. Mapping Variables**. At the prompt, *type* **22** and *press* *<ENTER>*. As the map unfolds you'll notice counties color coded according to percentage of increasing or decreasing population between 1980 and 1990. The lightest (yellow) clusters indicate areas where population is decreasing. The darker clusters denote the heaviest population increases. Refer back to the early map of Appalachia's three regions, either by looking in this manual or using the "Comp" (for comparison) function and *entering* **3**. The maps indicate that

people are leaving the _____ (Northern/Central/Southern) Appalachian region.

people are moving into the _____ (Northern/Central/Southern) region.

Press *<ENTER>* twice to return to the Percent Net Migration map and *Press* **L** (for legend). The legend shows two extremes in migration. The table should contain the following information

-44.2 <=Val<= -8.9	(79)
-8.8 <=Val<= -5.2	(76)
-5.1 <=Val<= -1.1	(84)
-1.0 <=Val<= 4.2	(78)
4.3 <=Val<= 90.3	(82)

The numbers in parentheses ( ) on the right reflect the numbers of counties in each category. Note that in the first category there are 79 counties in which somewhere between 44.2 and 8.9 percent of the people moved out of their county between 1980 and 1990. At the other extreme, there are 82 counties in which somewhere between 4.3 and 90.3 percent of the population moved in. *Press <ENTER>* to clear the legend from your screen and *press Name* and you'll see that Gwinnett County, GA led the region in migration with a percent of 90.3--it almost doubled its population! *Press the down arrow* and you'll see that Dawson, Ga. followed closely with a 85.3% increase. *Press the down arrow* again and you'll find another Georgia county---Georgia must be on a lot of people's minds!

To obtain a full list of migration in and out of all 399 Appalachian counties, *press* **D** (for distribution). You will find Georgia's Gwinnett County followed by:

1) __Gwinnett__   6) _____

2) _____   7) _____

3) _____   8) _____

4) _____   9) _____

5) _____   10) _____

Why might people moving to this part of Appalachia. Use the web to find out what makes northern Gwinnet, Dawson, Cherokee and Pike counties in Georgia so attractive. Summarize your findings here:

_____

_____

_____

_____

Contrast this list with the counties that <u>lost</u> the most population. *Arrow down* to the bottom of the list where Jackson, Alabama sits with a loss of 44.2 percent of its population. Look above Jackson and note the trend: which <u>three states</u>' Appalachian counties lost the most population?

1) _____

2) _____

3) _____

Why would Georgia gain population while these areas loose it? To answer such questions, researchers look for relationships (also called associations or correlations) between migration and other variables. Since common sense suggests that people follow employment opportunity, let's make a "scatterplot" of the relationship between migration and unemployment. *Select* **F. Scatterplot** from the **STATISTICAL ANALYSIS** menu. At the prompt for the <u>dependent variable</u> *type* **22** and *press* *<ENTER>*. At the prompt for the <u>independent variable</u>, *type* **37** and *press* *<ENTER>* twice. You'll get a graph that should look like this:

48

Figure 3.1

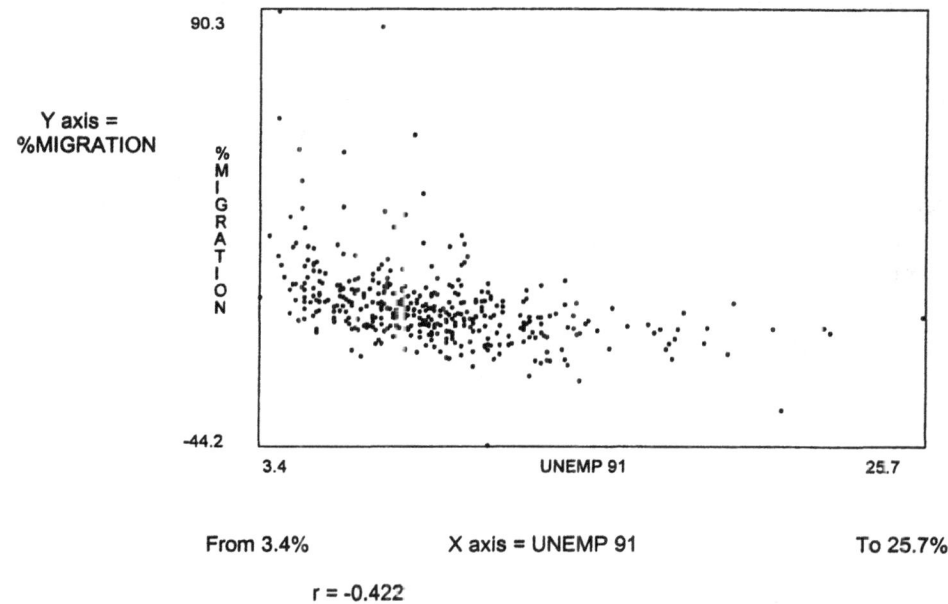

This scatterplot should look much better on your computer. To interpret the plot, you need to know the following terms and concepts:

1) <u>Cases</u>: Each dot represents a case. A case in this data is a county, therefore, there are 399 cases. Note the dots on the top, left hand side of the graph, indicating high in migration rates and low unemployment. They must be Gwinnett and Dawson counties in Georgia. *Type* S (for show case) and then *enter "Gwin."* The computer types the rest of the name and flashes its location on the graph. *Press <ENTER>* and *type Dawson*. It should be flashing right up there next to Gwinnett. What counties have high unemployment? Where would they be located on the graph? They would be found out along the X axis, on the right hand side of the plot. Notice that the dots on the right side are also relatively low on the vertical Y axis, suggesting that unemployment is associated with out migration (the percentage of people leaving a county between 1980 and 1990).

2) <u>Variables</u>: A variable is a characteristic that can change or vary from case to case. The variable which occurs first, or is suspected to cause change in the second variable is called the *independent* variable; the second or impacted variable is the *dependent* variable. In this example, the unemployment rate for 1991 (UNEMP 91) would be considered the independent variable and (%MIGRATION) the dependent variable.

3) The <u>X axis</u>. Scatterplots show the relationship of two variables to each other along two axes. The X axis is the *horizontal* measure for the first or "independent" variable. In the example in Figure 3.1, each case's score on the variable UNEMP 91 is located along the X axis, from 3.4 percent to 25.7 percent.

4) The Y axis is a vertical measure the second or "dependent" variable. In Figure 3.1, the dependent variable (%MIGRATION) is charted vertically from -44.2 to +90.3. Each county is plotted on the graph according to its scores on the independent and dependent variables.

5) Association and correlation: Look for the pattern of dots on the graph. The dots seem to descend from the left to the right. You can check this by letting the computer draw a straight line closest to all the dots. *Press <ENTER>* to leave the "show case" function and return to the scatterplot. *Press L (for line)* to draw the "regression line." It slopes down from left to right, indicating a *"negative association between the two variables."* When a line slopes down like this from left to right, it suggests that the higher the score on the independent variable(UNEMP91), the lower the score on the dependent variable (%MIGRATION). In this case, the dependent variable (%MIGRATION) ranges from -44.2% to +90.3, so the interpretation would be that higher unemployment is associated with out migration and lower unemployment (or higher employment and job opportunities) correlates with higher migration into a county. The line or "slope" suggesting a negative association looks like this:

Figure 3.2

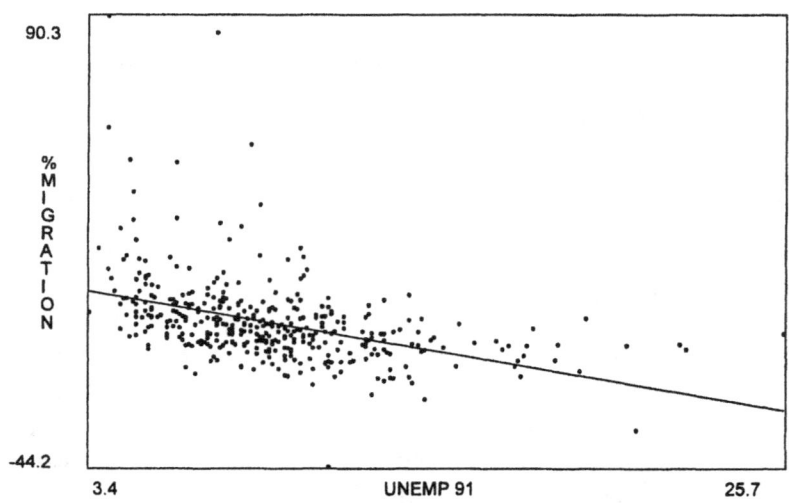

6) Outliers: Note that some dots (cases) stand out away from the cluster of dots in the left of the scatterplot. Cases that score farthest away from the average are called *"outliers."* The outliers in this example will tend to be at the top left and the bottom right of the graph. *Press O (for Outlier)* and you will see "Outlier: Dawson, GA" appear under the graph and the dot representing Dawson flash in red on the screen. As you would expect, it is in the upper left of the graph--higher in migration is associated with lower unemployment. Now the computer asks if you want to delete this outlier and tells you that if you do, the correlation "r" will change from -0.422 to -0.440 (meaning that eliminating this outlier for the data set makes the association between variables even stronger). *Press Y (for Yes!)* The computer should tell you that the next outlier is McDowell County, West Virginia. Notice its location on the lower right hand side of the graph--out migration is associated with high unemployment. *Press Y* again and you'll see the county with the highest unemployment, which is _____ (county, state). If you eliminate this county, the new r = _____. Continue to *Press Y* and you see a pattern suggesting in migration to Appalachian Georgia and parts of Pennsylvania and out migration from West Virginia.

50

7) <u>Slopes</u>: The data suggest that unemployment affects migration. We can *hypothesize* that unemployment may also have an association with poverty. *Press <ENTER> twice* to return to the SCATTERPLOT menu and *type* **39** for the dependent variable and **37** for the independent variable. When the graph appears you'll see that the axis X=UNEMP 91 and Y=%POOR89. *Press* **L** (for Line) and you'll see a *positive slope* indicating a positive relation between the two variables: Higher rates of unemployment are associated with higher rates of poverty; Pearson's r = 0.543. The scatterplot should look like this:

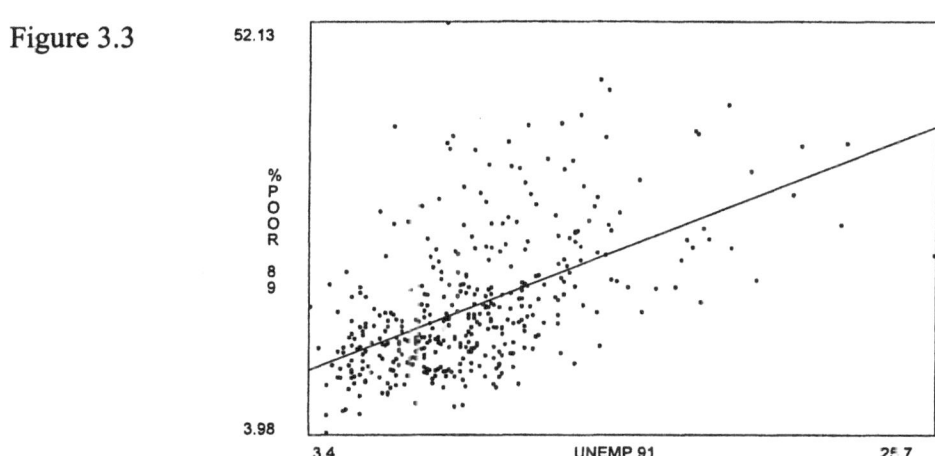

Figure 3.3

Figure 3.3 is an example of a <u>positive</u> slope, association and correlation. Figure 3.2 is an example of a <u>negative</u> slope, association and correlation. Once more, recreate the original unemployment/migration graph by *typing* **22** for the dependent variable and **37** for the independent variable. When the graph appears, *press* **L** (for Line) and again you will see an example of a negative slope. Incidentally, if the regression line doesn't go up or down, but stays horizontal and parallel to the x axis, it means there is no association between the two variables. In other words, as the scores on the independent variable increase, scores on the dependent variable stay the same; Pearson's r = 0.

Updating migration data: Government agencies such as the Census Bureau and the Appalachian Regional Commission are continually updating their data files. Shortly before this reprinting, the ARC published migration data for the 1990-1997 period. Did the trends of the 1980s continue in the 1990s?

Select **E. Mapping Variables**. At the prompt, *type* **94** and *press* *<ENTER>*. You will see a map indicating migration patterns for the 1990-1997 period. *Press* Comp. The screen will divide in two and take about 20 seconds to make a smaller map of the Appalachian region. You will be asked for the "Name or number of variable for comparison." *Enter* **22**. Another map will appear showing the migration patterns between 1980 and 1990.

    Do the maps look similar?   Yes   No   Not Sure

    What is the correlation coefficient r = _____

Press <ENTER> three times to return to the variable prompt and *type* **94**. After the map appears, *press* **D** and write down the ten counties with the highest in-migration in the 1990-1997 period. Compare your results by looking back a page 24 and seeing if these counties also ranked high on the 1980-1990 list.

        <u>1990- 1997</u>   <u>Rank Position in 1980-90 Migration</u>

1) _____   _____

2) _____   _____

3) _____   _____

4) _____   _____

5) _____   _____

6) _____   _____

7) _____   _____

8) _____   _____

9) _____   _____

10) _____   _____

Go to the bottom of the migration distribution list and record (from the bottom up) the counties losing the most population.

                399) _____

                398) _____

                397) _____

                396) _____

                395) _____

                394) _____

                393) _____

                392) _____

                391) _____

                390) _____

What might these counties might have in common the could spur out-migration?

_____

_____

_____

_____

Create a new scatterplot, using the new data for migration and unemployment rate for 1996. *Select* **F. Scatterplot** from the **STATISTICAL ANALYSIS** menu. At the prompt for the <u>dependent variable</u> *type* **94** and *press <ENTER>*. At the prompt for the <u>independent variable</u>, *type* **96** and *press <ENTER> twice* to bypass the subset request. When the scatterplot appears, *press* Line and *write in the labels for the* X AXIS *and the* Y AXIS *and draw in* the regression line:

Y AXIS

|
|
|
|
|
|
|
|
|
|_____ X AXIS

r = _____   Prob: _____   N: _____

Describe the <u>strength</u> (the correlation coefficient "r") and <u>direction</u> (positive or negative) of the relationship between unemployment and migration in the 1990-1997 period. Is this correlation stronger or weaker than the correlation for 1980-1990 (see Figure 3.1 on page 27)?

_____

_____

_____

_____

Review. This chapter introduces a number of new terms. Write out definitions for the following list in your own words. The glossary at the end of the book can help you, but writing descriptions out will help you make them part of your own *working knowledge*.

Case

Unit of analysis

Demographics

Population density

Metropolitan Statistical Area (MSA, CMSA, PMSA)

Migration

Correlation coefficient "r"

Levels (scales) of measurement:

Variable

Independent variable

Dependent variable

Categorical variables:

Continuous variable

X axis

Y axis

Strength of association between variables

Positive association between variables

Negative association between variables

You need to review these terms until you can explain them to yourself comfortably--until they become part of your working vocabulary. They will improve your ability to see relationships between variables and make choices. For example, if you didn't have strong ties to a particular place but wanted a good job, where would you go?

Georgia _____   Eastern Kentucky _____   West Virginia _____ (check one)

Use the scatterplot function to discover other variables your findings here, <u>using at least six of the terms listed above</u> to explain your findings. For example, you could report on the relationship between migration and the percentage of the labor force involved in manufacturing -- or mining.

Now that you see how data can help us understand the relationships between variables such as unemployment, poverty and migration, you're ready to begin an analysis of Appalachia's economy.

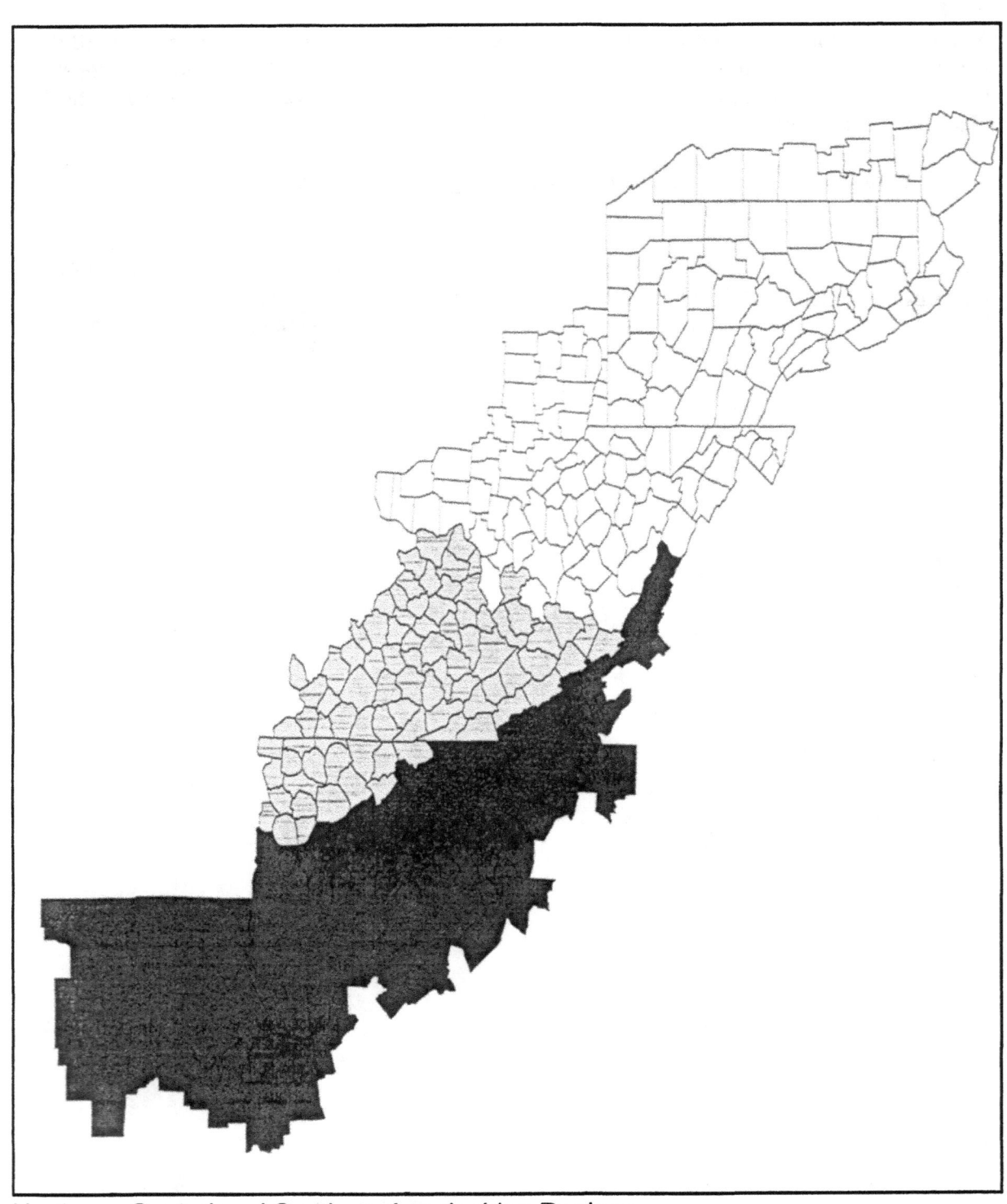

Northern, Central and Southern Appalachian Regions

V. The Appalachian Economy I: Comparing Subregions

Analysis of Variance (ANOVA) in Group Scores

In the last chapter we explored the association of migration in and out of Appalachian counties with economic factors such as unemployment. Maps and scatterplots were the statistical tools employed in the exploration process. We can use another tool called *analysis of variance*, to compare migration by the three Appalachian subregions--the North, Central and Southern.

From the STATISTICAL ANALYSIS MENU select **C. Analysis of Variance**. At the dependent variable prompt, *type 22 (or %migration) and press <ENTER>*. At the independent variable prompt, *enter 3 (or "Three Regn," an abbreviation for Three Regions) and press <ENTER> twice (bypassing the request for a subset variable)*. You will see the following graph:

Figure 4.1

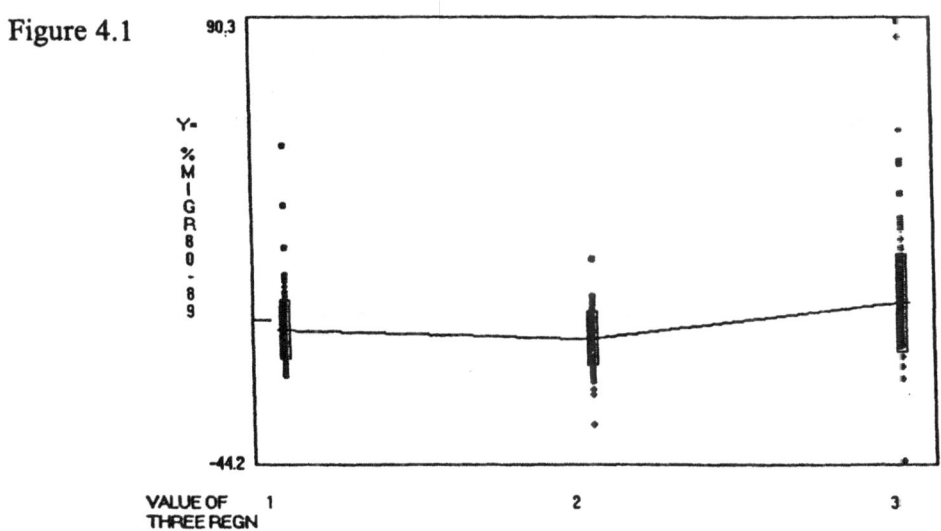

What you see on the computer monitor should be superior to Figure 4.1. *Press X for the x axis variable label.* It tells you that the horizontal axis "Three Regn" (three regions) is broken into three groups: 1) North, 2) Central and 3) Southern Appalachian subregions. Each dot represents a single county. The counties are clustered vertically in three columns by subregion and run up or down the plot according to their in or out migration percentage. The rectangular boxes are indicators of the spread of variance in individual county scores from their group (region's) average or mean score, which is marked by the horizontal line in the middle of the box. A taller box means that a group's scores are more widely spread. The boxes mark the spread of scores one *standard deviation* above and below the mean score, which includes approximately the 68 percent of that group's cases closest to the average score. The dots at the extreme top and bottom of the columns represent *outliers*. The line running horizontally across the chart connects the *means* for each group. Notice how the line slopes down between Groups 1 and 2 and slopes up between Groups 2 and 3. Since Group 2 is Central Appalachia, this region must have the lowest mean score. Southern Appalachia has the highest. *Press <ENTER> to continue.*

Press **M** (for means) and you'll find the average migration score for each region in the following table:

Table 4.1   N: 399 (counties/cases)   Missing (counties/cases):   0

Region	N (number of counties)	Mean (Average % migration)
North	144	-4.344
Central	84	-7.005
Southern	171	4.046

Central Appalachia had the most out migration (-7.005). The Northern region also lost population, while the Southern gained it. Why would people want to leave Central Appalachia? Might it be a lack of jobs? *Press <ENTER>* and, at the dependent variable prompt, *type* **37)UNEMP 91**. *Enter* **3)Three Regn** for the independent variable. Note the line connecting the mean scores for each group; it seems like an inversion of the previous plot: Central Appalachia has the highest mean score for unemployment and the Southern region had the lowest. *Press* **M** (for Mean) *and record the scores below:*

Table 4.2   N: 399 (counties/cases)   Missing (counties/cases):   0

Region	N (number of counties)	Mean (Average % unemployment)
North	144	
Central	84	
Southern	171	

Describe your results: Which region has the highest unemployment? The lowest?

Compare Appalachia's three regions according to the following dependent variables:

1. 32) PERCAP 92 by 3) Three Regions

When the table appears, *type* **Y** *and write in* the long label for PERCAP 92 here:

_____

Press **M** *(for Mean) and record the scores below:*

Region	Mean (PERCAP 92)
North	
Central	
Southern	

Convert the numbers under "Mean (PERCAP92)" into dollars and *round off* to the nearest dollar ($15,249). Describe your findings, region by region. (This may seem a little tedious, but this is part of data analysis).

Do one more procedure before leaving this table: press **A** for ANOVA (analysis of variance). Write in the numbers for the

F = _____   p (probability) = _____ E^2 = _____

These figures will explained in more detail at the end of the chapter (page 71). Basically, the **F** ratio is a measure of how much of the variation in scores occurs *within* each region as compared to *between* the three regions. The higher the F ratio, the bigger the differences between regions. The "**p** value" or probability is an indication of our chances of being wrong in claiming the difference in scores between the regions is "statistically significant." To be significant, the probability of being wrong must be less than 1 chance in 20 or .05. The **Eta square** ("E^2") indicates how much of the variance in the dependent variable (PERCAP 92) is explained by the independent variable "Three Region."

Go back in time to 1981 and record per capita income in 1981: *Enter* variable 88) PERCAP 81 by variable 3) THREE REGN

When the table appears, *type* **Y** *and write in* the long label for PERCAP 81:

_____

Press **M** (for Mean) *and record the scores below:*

Region	Mean (PERCAP 81)
North	
Central	
Southern	

Remember to round off and convert to dollars.

Now update your findings to 1995. Try variable 92) PERCAP 95 by 3) Three Regions:

When the table appears, *type* **Y** *and write in* the long label for PERCAP 95:

_____

Press **M** (for Mean) *and record the scores below:*

Region	Mean (PERCAP 95)
North	
Central	
Southern	

Describe your results. Can you find any trends from 1981 to 1992 to 1995?

2. **27) H.S.GRAD90 by 3) THREE REGN**

When the table appears, *type* **Y** *and write in* the long label here:

_____

Press **M** (for Mean) *and record the scores below:*

Region	Mean (H.S. Grad90)
North	
Central	
Southern	

Sometimes decision makers want to know how much more one percentage or rate is over another. They compute this by subtracting one rate from the other, dividing by whichever is the "base rate" being used for comparison and then multiplying by 100 to convert the ratio into a percentage. In this case, if we want to know how much the North's mean education rate is higher than the Central Region rate, we would compute:

$$\frac{\text{North - Central}}{\text{Central}} = \frac{41.595 - 30.039}{30.079} = \frac{11.516}{30.079} = 0.3828 \times 100 = 38.29\%$$

The North's mean percentage of those 25 and over who have a high school degree is 38.29 percent higher than of the Central subregion.

This method of portraying differences between rates is commonly used by public health officials. *Practice this technique in each of the exercises in the rest of the chapter.*

Write in the numbers for the

F = _____   p (probability) = _____ E^2 = _____

3. **41) POOR FAM89 by 3) THREE REGN**

When the table appears, *type* **Y** *and write in* the long label here:

_____

Press **M** *(for Mean) and record the scores below:*

Region	Mean (POOR FAM89)
North	
Central	
Southern	

Anything interesting? The Central subregion's mean score is ____ percent above that of the North subregion. Describe your results:

Write in the numbers for the

F = _____   p (probability) = _____ E^2 = _____

4: **53)** MANUF.$90 by 3) THREE REGN

When the table appears, *type* **Y** *and write in* the long label:

_____

Press **M** *and record the scores below:*

Region	Mean (MANUF.$90)
North	
Central	
Southern	

The North subregion's mean salary in manufacturing is _____ percent above that of the Central subregion. Describe your results:

Write in the numbers for the

    F = _____   p (probability) = _____ E^2 = _____

5: **56)** RETAIL $90 by 3) THREE REGN

When the table appears, *type Y and write in* the long label:

_____

Enter the mean scores:

Region	Mean (RETAIL $90)
North	
Central	
Southern	

The North subregion's mean salary in retail sales is only _____ percent above that of the Central subregion. Describe your results:

Write in the numbers for the

F = _____   p (probability) = _____ E^2 = _____

6: 59) SERVICES$90 by 3) THREE REGN

When the table appears, *type* **Y** *and write in* the long label:

_____

Enter the mean scores:

Region	Mean (SERVICES$90)
North	
Central	
Southern	

The North subregion's mean salary in services is only _____ percent above that of the Southern subregion. Describe your results:

Write in the numbers for the

F = _____   p (probability) = _____ E^2 = _____

7: **51**) % MINE EM90 by 3) THREE REGN

When the table appears, *type* **Y** *and write in* the long label:

_____

Enter the mean scores:

Region	Mean (%MINE EM90)
North	
Central	
Southern	

Describe these very interesting results, using percentage differences comparisons between the Northern and Central regions and the Central and Southern regions.

Write in the numbers for the

F = _____   p (probability) = _____ E^2 = _____

8: **54**) %MANUF.E90 by 3) THREE REGN

When the table appears, *type* **Y** *and write in* the long label:

_____

Enter the mean scores:

Region	Mean (%MANUF.E90)
North	
Central	
Southern	

The Northern subregion's mean percentage of people employed in manufacturing is _____ percent above that of the Central subregion. Describe your results:

Write in the numbers for the

F = _____   p (probability) = _____ E^2 = _____

9: **66**) FARM VAL87 by 3) THREE REGN

When the table appears, *type* **Y** *and write in* the long label:

Enter the mean scores:

Region	Mean (FARM VAL87)
North	
Central	
Southern	

The Northern subregion's mean farm value is ____ percent above that of the Central subregion. Describe your results:

Write in the numbers for the

F = _____   p (probability) = _____ E^2 = _____

9: **45)** DR.RATE90 by 3) THREE REGN

When the table appears, *type* **Y** *and write in* the long label:

_____

Enter the mean scores:

Region	Mean (DR.RATE90)
North	
Central	
Southern	

The Northern subregion's mean value for active nonfederal physicians per 100,000 is _____ percent above that of the Central subregion. Describe your results: Are there some outliers in the Northern region that might exaggerate their rate?

Write in the numbers for the

$F = $ _____ p (probability) = _____ $E^2 = $ _____

10: **44)** INFANT90-2 by 3) THREE REGN

When the table appears, *type Y and write in* the long label:

_____

Enter the mean scores:

Region	Mean (INFANT90-2)
North	
Central	
Southern	

How do these results differ from previous findings? What other factors (variables) might explain this difference?

Write in the numbers for the

F = _____   p (probability) = _____ E^2 = _____

In the past ten exercises, we have focused on comparing the mean scores of the three subregions (categories of the independent variable) for a number of dependent variables (infant mortality rates, families in poverty in 1989, etc.). **Analysis of Variance (ANOVA)** provides additional statistical tools to assess the impact of the categories of the independent variable on the scores of the dependent variable. If you are using this text in a statistics course, your instructor will explain ANOVA in detail. Briefly, the analysis of variance procedure indicates how much of the variance between all the scores (399 scores/counties in our data set) is explained by an independent variable. For example, how much of the poverty in an Appalachian county can be explained by the fact that it is located in the Central Appalachian subregion? ANOVA computations lead to an "F ratio," in which the numerator is a measure of the differences between group (Appalachian subregion) average (mean) scores and the denominator is a measure of the differences in the case/county scores within each group. In the form of an equation

$$\frac{\text{differences between group means}}{\text{differences between scores within groups}} = F$$

If the independent variable accounts for or explains much of the variance in scores, the F will be large: 50/2=25. If the groups means are pretty close to each other and most of the variance is within the groups, the F will be small: 2/50=.04. *Return to* variable 41)POOR FAM 89, as an example, for the dependent variable and 3)Three Region as the independent variable. When you get the bar and whisker plot, *press* **A** (for ANOVA). You will find the F ratio=118.152. That's a high score, which suggests that much of the variance in scores is a result of the location of a county in a particular subregion. The **Eta square** ("E^2") indicates that 0.374 (37.4 percent) of the variance is explained by the independent variable "Three Region."

Repeat the procedure for **53)MANUF.$90.** F = _____ E^2 = _____

What percentage of the variance in manufacturing salaries is explained by a county's location in a particular region? The answer is E^2 multiplied by 100: _____

Find the F ratio for variable **27)H.S.GRAD90**   F = _____ E^2 = _____

How much of the variance in the percentage of people over 25 with a high school diploma is explained by a county's location in a particular region _____

Find the F ratio for variable **44)INFANT 90-92** F = _____ E^2 = _____

How much of the variance in the three year infant mortality rate is explained by a county's location in a particular region? _____

In summary, you can see that a county's location in one of Appalachia's subregions makes a difference in manufacturing salaries, poverty and educational opportunity, but not in infant mortality rates.

You can continue your comparison of Appalachia's three subregions with **tables,** which explore relationships between two categorical variables: *Press <ENTER>* until you return to the STATISTICAL ANALYSIS menu and *select* **B. Tabular Statistics.** At the prompt for the row variable *type* **87)DISTRSDCOLL,** which is a measurement of the overall economic condition of counties as assessed by the Appalachian Regional Commission in 1988. The counties are ranked from "severely distressed" at the low end to "strong/very strong." For the column variable, *enter* **3)THREE REGN** to break the county economic rankings down by the North, Central and Southern subregions. *Press <ENTER>* twice to bypass requests for control variables and subsets. When the **table** appears, look carefully at the number of severely distressed counties in the three subregions. Of the 144 counties in the North region, 13 are severely distressed, as are 26 of 171 Southern counties. But the Central Appalachia has 50 severely distressed counties out of its total of 84. It's easier to compare these numbers if you convert them to percentages. *Press* **C** (for column percentages) and enter the results below:

North___9.0%___   Central_____   Southern_____

Central Appalachia's economic difficulty is obvious. Try one more table. *Press <ENTER>* to return to a new request for a row prompt and *enter* **86)PC%US92col.** This is a comparison of each county's average income with the national average. If a county per capita income scored as 100% of the U.S. average, it would be the same as the U.S. average. If it scored 125%, it would be 25% higher than the national average. If it scored 50%, its average (mean) income would be half of the U.S. average. To find out how Central Appalachia compares to the other two subregions, *enter* **3)THREE REGN** again as the column variable. *Press <ENTER>* twice and, when the table appears, *type* C to obtain the column percentages (which appear in blue). Write in the percentage of counties in each region with incomes of only 45-60% of the national average.

North_____   Central_____   Southern_____

Describe your results:

In this chapter, you have learned about some differences between the three Appalachian subregions and about two statistical tools helpful in analyzing those differences: Analysis of Variance (ANOVA) and tabular statistics. Future chapters will provide more information about these statistical tools and when to use them. For the moment, concentrate on what you have discovered about Appalachia by ***writing a comparative summary of the economic status of its three subregions***. Cite the data you have generated on the previous pages! Compare dependent variables such as per capita income and mean (average) pay in manufacturing as they differ across the three subregions. Use the new tools at your disposal: percentages more or less; F ratios, probability scores for statistical significance and Eta square (E^2).

VI. The Economy II: Industry and Opportunity
Correlations and Regressions

> Bivariate analysis explores the relation between two variables. Different tools are employed in bivariate analysis, depending on whether the variables are **categorical** or continuous.
>
> **Analysis of Variance** (ANOVA) can be employed when the dependent variable is **continuous**, for example, a number, rate or percentage as in variable 22 (%MIGRATION), and the independent variable is **categorical**, such as 3)Three regions, which has three values or categories: 1) Northern, 2) Central and 3) Southern. *The last chapter focused on ANOVA and the comparison of means.*
>
> When both variables are **categorical**, for example, variable 3) Three Regions by variable 6)CITY, whose values are 1)Metro and 2)Nonmetro, *tables* are employed. *We work with tables in the next chapter (VII).*
>
> When both variables are **continuous**, such as variable 22)%MIGRATION by 33)PCAP%US92, *correlations, scatterplots* and *regressions* are employed. *We work with correlations and regressions in this chapter.*
>
> Note that on the MicroCase statistical analysis menu, selection "B" is for tables, "C" is ANOVA, and options "F" through "I" offer a range of tools for the examination of relationships between continuous variables: scatterplots, correlations, regressions and multiple regressions.

Comparative data explored in the previous chapter found real differences in income, education and services between the three Appalachian subregions. Continuous variables such as per capita income and percentage of people over 25 who have completed high school were compared across three categories: Northern, Central and Southern Appalachian regions. But there also appeared to be relationships between the continuous variables: For example, Central Appalachia had the highest unemployment rates and the lowest high school graduation rates. Might these two continuous variables be associated with each other?

From the STATISTICAL ANALYSIS menu, select **F. Scatterplot.** *Type* **37** (UNEMP 91) for the dependent variable and 27 (H.S.GRAD90) for the independent variable and *press <ENTER> twice.* After the scatterplot appears, *press* L to obtain the regression line. Notice that the line is almost flat, indicating no significant relationship between unemployment and percentage of people completing high school. Regression lines enable you to quickly assess the *strength* and *direction* of an association between two variables by the steepness of its slope: a horizontal line indicates that as the independent variable increases nothing happens to the dependent variable--it stays the same. So the steeper the *slope*, the stronger the relationship. If the slope goes from the lower left of the plot to the upper right, it is called a "***major diagonal***" and the relationship is *positive*: the *higher* the high school graduation rate, the *higher* the unemployment rate. If the regression line moves down from the upper left towards the lower right, it is a "***minor diagonal***" and the association is *negative*: the *higher* the high school graduation rate, the *lower* the unemployment rate. Continuing our analysis of the Appalachian economy, we might hypothesize a relationship between mean county education level and unemployment rates: the higher percentage of people with a high school diploma, the lower the unemployment rate. Let's see:

Figure 5.1. 1991 County Unemployment Rates by percentage of people over 25 with High School Degrees.

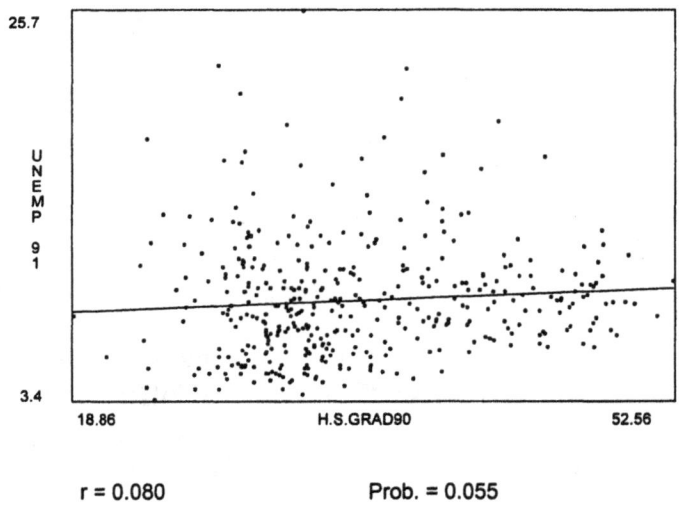

r = 0.080   Prob. = 0.055

Note the flat regression line--almost horizontal--and that the correlation coefficient "r" is only 0.080. It should be at least 0.10 to suggest even a weak relationship. You may recall from Chapter II (page 16) statistician William Fox's *rough* measures for strength of association between variables.

$r \geq .70$ Very strong relationship

$.50 \leq r < .70$ Strong relationship

$.20 \leq r < .50$ Moderate relationship

$.10 \leq r < .20$ Weak relationship

$r < .10$ Negligible relationship

> By the way, what is that "Prob. = 0.055" below Graph 5.1? "Prob." stands for probability: the probability or chances of being wrong. It's used when someone has taken a *sample* from a larger *population* and wants to know if the relationship found in the sample can be *generalized* to the entire population. If our 399 county data set was a random sample of all the counties in the United States, we would use the probability measure to determine if the relationship found between two variables in the sample is "significant" enough for us to claim that it also exists in the population. If the probability score is 0.05 or less, researchers are willing to say that the relationship found in the sample is *significant* and will be found in the population. The chances of their being wrong in that claim and that there is no relationship between variables are less than five out of 100, or one in 20.
>
> The smaller the probability or "p value," the stronger the claim to the validity of the association between two variables. Often, the computer will say that Prob. = 0.00. Rather than report there is no chance of error, we say $p < .001$, that the probability of error is less than one in a thousand.
>
> When researchers have data for an entire population as we have here with all of Appalachia's counties, they conduct significance tests to assess the chances of a score for a correlation coefficient (or other measure) being caused by random processes.

Create your own scatterplot, this time looking at unemployment in 1980 (**38**: UNEMP 80) as the dependent variable and median school years education completed by people in Appalachian counties over 25 years of age (**29**: MED.EDUC80) as the independent variable. (The median education variable was not available for 1990, so I had to move back to the previous census.)

    1) Describe the *slope and direction of the regression line* (positive or negative; steep or gradual):

    _____

    2) The Pearson Product-Moment Correlation r = _____ .

    3) This tells us that the higher the level of education, the higher/lower (circle one) the unemployment rate.

    4) Therefore, the relationship between the two variables is strong/moderate/weak (circle one), positive/negative (circle one).

    5) The probability ("prob.") of error in saying we have a relationship between educational level and unemployment is _____ .

You now have the data you need to *report your findings*. For example, in this case you would report "there was a <u>moderate</u>, <u>negative</u> correlation between mean county educational level and unemployment in 1980, $r = -.27$, $p > .001$. The higher the educational level, the lower the unemployment rate." The "p value" or probability indicates that virtually no chance (stated as less than one chance in a thousand) that our correlation is due to random causes.

Researchers are often asked to suggest relationships between variables *before* the research is conducted. A statement about a possible relationship between variables is called a *hypothesis* (literally "little thesis"). Thus we can initially *hypothesize* that "There is a strong, positive association between per capita income and level of educational attainment in Appalachian counties." Usually, hypotheses are flipped around to suggest that there is *no* association between variables. These are called *null hypotheses,* positing "null" or no relationship between variables. In this example we would say, "There is *no* relationship between per capita income and level of educational attainment in Appalachian counties." Let's see if we can reject our null hypothesis. *Enter* **32)PERCAP 92** as the dependent variable and **29)MED.EDUC80** as the independent variable.

> We find that there is/is not (choose one) a _____, _____
> relationship between per capita income and median education (r = _____,
> p >0.001).
>
> We--reject--fail to reject--(choose one) the null hypothesis!

Note that, although the data tells us that p = 0.000, it's better to say there's always a chance of the correlation coefficient being the result of random factors, even if it's only one in a thousand–1/1000--0.001!

In the last chapter, you found that the economic indicator rates for Central Appalachia varied considerably from the other two subregions. Its economy was marked by more mining and less manufacturing, lower levels of education and services and higher levels of poverty and unemployment. With correlation analysis, we can further explore the association between these two continuous variables. On the SCATTERPLOT menu, *type in* **37)UNEMP91** for the dependent variable and **51)%MINE EM90** as the independent variable. I'll duplicate the graph here:

Figure 5.2. 1991 Unemployment Rate and Percentage of Labor Force in Mining.

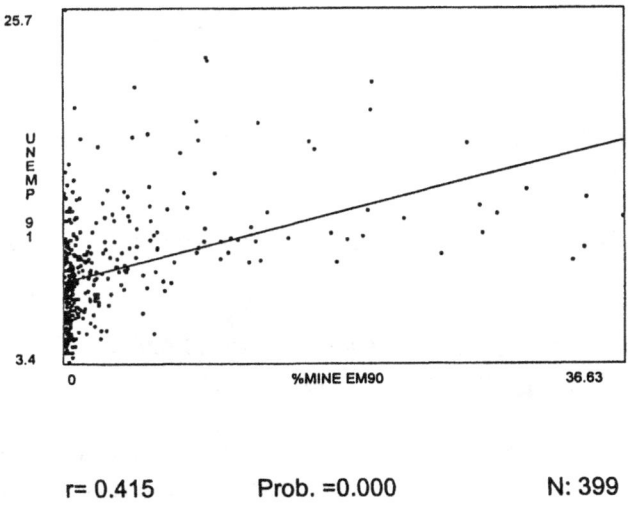

r= 0.415   Prob. =0.000   N: 399

Notice how most of the cases cluster on the lower left; there is little or no mining in most of Appalachia's counties. Also note the positive slope and that r = 0.415. We can reject the null hypothesis of no relationship between mining and unemployment: there is a solid, moderate, positive association between the two variables.

WAIT JUST A MINUTE! MIGHT ALL THOSE NON-MINING COUNTIES, STACKED UP LIKE A BAD CASE OF ACNE IN THE LOWER LEFT HAND CORNER OF THE PLOT, EXAGGERATE THE RELATIONSHIP BETWEEN UNEMPLOYMENT AND THE PERCENTAGE OF THE WORK FORCE EMPLOYED IN MINING?

Well...hmm. Since we know that most of the mining occurs in Central Appalachia (see page 42), we can use the *subset* function to narrow our focus to its 84 counties. Again, on the SCATTERPLOT menu, *type in* **37)UNEMP 91** for the dependent variable and **51)%MINE EM90** as the independent variable. When asked for the "name or number of variable 1 for defining subset," *enter* **3**. The computer says we have chosen "3) Three Regn," and that its low value is 1 and its high value is 3. It then asks for the *lower limit. Type in* **2**. The computer says that 2 stands for the Central region and asks for the *upper limit. Type in* **2** *again and press <ENTER> twice* to bypass the second request for a subset. With the regression line added, your graph should look like this:

Figure 5.3. 1991 Central Appalachian counties' unemployment by percentage of labor force employed in the mines.

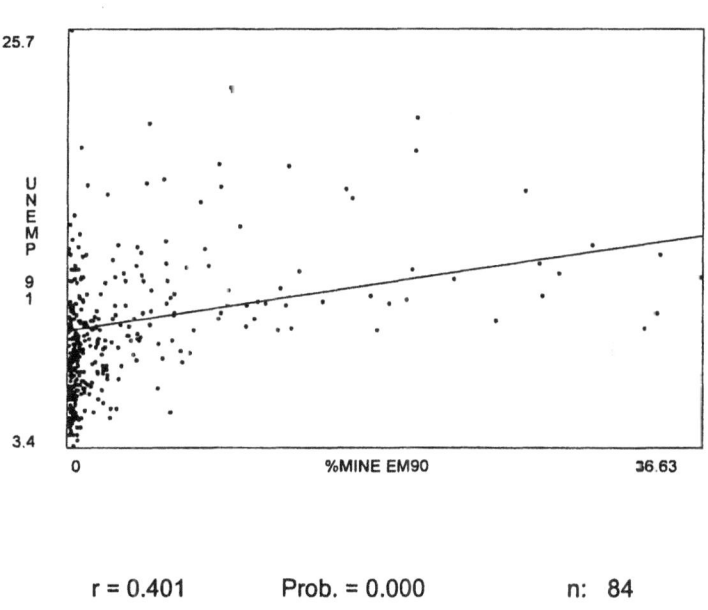

r = 0.401   Prob. = 0.000   n: 84

What does it show? The Central Appalachian subset of 84 counties has a correlation coefficient $r = 0.401$. There still is a moderate, positive relationship saying that higher percentages of workers engaged in mining is associated with higher levels of unemployment. (And a *subset* is a group or groups selected out from a variable containing a larger number of groups.)

Let's continue our analysis by exploring the relationship between mining and poverty. *Press <ENTER>* until you return to the STATISTICAL ANALYSIS menu. *Select* **G. Correlation**. This selection gives you the Pearson Product-Moment Correlation r for as many variables as you'd like to explore at one time. The easiest way to select your variables is to use the F3 key. *Press* **F3** and use the down arrow to move down the list of variables. *Select* **51) %MINE EM91** *with the left arrow key, then use the up arrow and left arrow again to select* **39)%POOR 89; 41) POOR FAM89** and **43)CHLD POOR89**. (The right arrow key provides the long label for each variable.) *Press <ENTER>* twice to bypass another the prompt for a fifth variable and the subset request. You will see a *correlation matrix* in which each variable is correlated with every other variable.

	51)%MINE EM9	39)%POOR 89	41)POOR FAM89	43)CHLD POR89
51)%MINE EM90	1.000	0.478**	0.513**	0.473**
	(399)	(399)	(399)	(399)
39)%POOR 89	0.478**	1.000	0.986**	0.971**
	(399)	(399)	(399)	(399)
41)POOR FAM89	0.513**	0.986**	1.000	0.970**
	(399)	(399)	(399)	(399)
43)CHLD POR89	0.473**	0.971**	0.970**	1.000
	(399)	(399)	(399)	(399)

The first column (columns run up and down; rows left to right) provides the correlations (r) we're after. Note that $r = 1.000$ in the first cell; that's because %MINE EM90 correlates perfectly with itself. (A line of 1.000 scores goes diagonally down the matrix, as variables are correlated with themselves. This is computer junk! Ignore it. Just use the correlations listed below the 1.000 line.) Note also that the (399) entries are a reflection of the number of cases (399 Appalachian counties). Now that you see how a matrix works, look at how the percentage of the workforce involved in mining correlates with the percentage of poor people in a county: $r = 0.478$. The correlation is 0.513 with poor families and 0.473 with poor children. We can conclude that all of these measures of poverty have a consistent, strong, positive association with mining in Appalachia.(Remember that "positive" does not mean "good," but rather tells of the direction of the relationship between the two variables: as one goes up, so does the other. In a negative relationship, as one variable goes up, the other goes down. Think of the slope of a regression line in a scatterplot.)

Why should a vigorous, productive activity like mining be associated with unemployment and poverty? Your instructor can refer you to a number of sources about the history of mining and corporate activity in the Central Appalachian coal fields. Some authors to explore in an initial search in your school library or on the Internet are Ronald D Eller, Helen Lewis, John Gaventa and Steve Fisher. If you live in a coal mining area, you might talk with some miners and coal mine owners.

Is the relationship of mining to factors such as poverty and unemployment unique? What about other areas of the economy: manufacturing, retail and services? Construct a correlation matrix for **54)%MANUF.E90, 37)** UNEM 91, **39)** POOR 89; **41)** POOR FAM and **43)** POOR CHILD. List the correlations below:

	54)%MANUF.E90
37) UNEMP 91	r =
39) POOR 89	r =
41) POOR FAM89	r =
43) CHLD POOR89	r =

Explain these results, remembering that a minus sign (-) indicates a negative (or inverse) relationship between variables. (An inverse relationship is one where the score on the dependent variable decreases as the independent variable increases.)

Construct the same matrix again, only this time *select* Central Appalachia as a *subset*. At the "enter a list of variables" prompt, type in **54)%MANUF.E90, 37)UNEM 91, 39)POOR 89, 41)POOR FAM** and **43) POOR CHILD**. Press <ENTER> and, at the subset prompt, *type* **3** and then **2** for both low and high values. List the correlations below

	54)%MANUF.E90
37) UNEMP 91	r =
39) POOR 89	r =
41) POOR FAM89	r =
43) CHLD POOR89	r =

Surprise! I bet you didn't expect this. Compare these results to the previous table:

Construct the same matrix for the North subregion. At the subset prompt, *type* 3 and then 1 for both low and high values. List the correlations below:

	54)%MANUF.E90
37) UNEMP 91	r =
39) POOR 89	r =
41) POOR FAM89	r =
43) CHLD POOR89	r =

Remember the federal government's description of the North subregion as having an old and outmoded manufacturing base? Manufacturing here is not having the same positive impact it appears to be having in Central Appalachian counties.

Let's see how poverty associates with different kinds of economies. Variables 50) MINING %90; 52)MANUFCT%90; 55) RETAIL%90 AND 58) SERVICES%90 report the earnings from mining, manufacturing, retail and services as a percentage of a county's overall income. Some counties will have much more manufacturing, for example. Does more of one kind of economy associate with less poverty---do different economic bases carry different economic life chances? At the CORRELATION menu prompts for variables, *type* **39, 50, 52, 55, 58**. *Enter the results* in the following table:

	39) %POOR
50) MINING %90	r =
52) MANUFCT%90	r =
55) RETAIL%90	r =
58) SERVICES%90	r =

Mining is positively/negatively (choose one) associated with poverty and the relationship is weak/moderate/strong (choose one). With r = 0.032, **retailing** has no association with **poverty**. **Manufacturing** has a strong/moderate/weak (choose one), positive/negative (choose one) association with poverty, while **services** have a _____(Fill in the blank) relationship. In summary, it appears that the two economic areas with the strongest correlation with poverty are _____ and _____.

In this chapter, you have used scatterplots, regression lines and correlations to explore the relationships between education, types of economies, unemployment and poverty. You have learned how to use hypotheses and a correlation matrix.

If you were a county commissioner or planner, what kind of economic base would you want for your constituents? If the software is available, put together a Microsoft PowerPoint or Corel Presentations slide show, showing the advantages and disadvantages of different economic development plans. (My students enjoy presenting their plans to each other and other faculty.)

VII: Voting Patterns and Economic Conditions

Tables, χ^2, and Nonparametric Measures of Association

In previous chapters, we have analyzed relationships between continuous, numerical variables (frequencies, rates and percentages) and between continuous and categorical variables, such as 3)THREE REGN and 6)CITY. We sought to discover associations among continuous variables with **scatterplots, correlations** and **regressions**. We broke down continuous variables by the values of a categorical variable, with **analysis of variance (ANOVA)**. Now we will use **tabular analysis** to explore relationships between two categorical variables.

Let's begin by constructing some tables showing voting by Appalachian subregion. From the red STATISTICAL ANALYSIS menu, select **B. Tabular Statistics**. At the "Enter the name or number of the row variable" prompt, *type* **83)**PRES.VT92. *Press <ENTER>*. At the column variable prompt, *enter* **3)**THREE REGN. *Press <ENTER> three times* to bypass the request for a control variable and a subset variable. You will see a table with the following information:

Table 7.1. Counties voting Republican or Democratic in the 1992 presidential election broken down by the three Appalachian subregions.

	North	Central	Southern	TOTAL
DEMOCRATIC	66	53	66	185
REPUBLICAN	76	30	103	209
Missing	2	1	2	5
TOTAL	142	83	169	394

The table tells us that of the 142 counties reporting in the North subregion, 66 went Democratic and 76 Republican. There is no data on two counties. For the Central region, 53 went Democratic and 30 Republican and in the Southern region it was 66 and 103. In the TOTAL column on the right, we see that the Democrats took 185 counties in Appalachia as a whole and the Republicans beat them with 209. It appears that the Republicans did better in the North and Southern subregions while the Democrats carried the Central subregion. But this is a table of raw numbers or what researchers call "**frequencies.**" The problem with frequencies is that it's hard to make comparisons between the different regions. What does "66" mean when compared to "53?" If frequencies are converted to **percentage ratios**, where each column totals 100 (instead of 142--83-169), making comparisons is easy.

Press **Col.%** (column percentages). Below the frequencies you'll see the percentages appear, color coded in blue.

Table 7.2: Frequencies and percentages of counties voting Republican or Democratic in the 1992 presidential election, broken down by the three Appalachian subregions.

	North	Central	Southern	TOTAL
DEMOCRATIC	66	53	66	185
% Democratic	46.5	63.9	39.1	47.0
REPUBLICAN	76	30	103	209
% Republican	53.5	36.1	60.9	53.0
Missing	2	1	2	5
TOTAL (frequencies)	142	83	169	394
TOTAL (Percent)	100.0	100.0	100.0	100.0

The percentages immediately enable us to make comparisons. In 1992, the Democrats carried 46.5% of the North counties, 63.9% of the Central and 39.1 % of the Southern. They're stronger in Central Appalachia, but the Republicans carried 53 percent of the region as a whole. Have these percentages changed over time? Remember Ronald Reagan? He was elected president in 1980. How did the Republicans do when he led their party?

Select **B. Tabular Statistics**. At the "Enter the name or number of the row variable" prompt, *type* **80)PRES.VT80**. *Press <ENTER>*. At the column variable prompt, *type* **3)THREE REGN**. *Press <ENTER> three times to bypass the request for a control variable and a subset variable. Enter only the percentages* (listed in yellow) *below:*

Table 7.3: **Percentages** of counties voting Republican or Democratic in the 1980 presidential election, broken down by the three Appalachian subregions.

Percentage of counties voting:	North	Central	Southern
DEMOCRATIC	26.1		
REPUBLICAN			
TOTAL	100.0	100.0	100.0

Comparing the percentages found in Table 7.2 to those in Table 7.3, we find that the subregion that had the highest percentage change between 1980 and 1992 was the

Northern -- Central -- Southern (circle one), with a difference of _____ percent.

Why might voters in this region have changed party allegiance between 1980 and 1992? Did anything happen to the economy or political life of the nation to prompt this switch? If so, why might the chosen party policies be preferable, given the change in economic fortunes?

Let's look at the Republicans. Did the voters like Ronald Reagan in 1984, after his first four years in office? *Enter* **81** as the row variable and **3** as the column variable and *fill in* the cells in Table 7.4.

Table 7.4: Percentages of counties voting Republican or Democratic in the 1984 presidential election, broken down by the three Appalachian subregions.

Percentage of counties voting:	North	Central	Southern
DEMOCRATIC			
REPUBLICAN			
TOTAL	100	100	100

Hmm. If I were the president, with these results, I'd be pretty _____

_____!

Are there differences in voting patterns between the three subregions? Remember Central Appalachia has been dominated by a single industry--the coal industry, with a long history of conflict between working people and large corporations that control land, resources and often local government, including law enforcement. It is not surprising that residents would support a political party with a more activist view of the federal government working to protect the environment and the rights and well being of blue collar workers. You have also seen in chapters 1 and 4 that Central Appalachia is, economically, the worst off of the three regions. Do counties in increasingly difficult economic straits favor the Democrats? Let's *hypothesize* (make an educated guess of) a positive correlation between increasing economic distress and support for the Democrats--that higher percentages of distressed counties will vote Democratic.

> The Appalachian Regional Commission's **Distressed Counties Program** began in 1983 to provide special funding for the region's poorest counties. To qualify for Distressed County status, a county must have an unemployment rate at least 150% of the U.S. rate of 5.7 (8.6% or higher), 150% of the U.S. poverty rate of 13.1% (19.7% or higher) and less than 67% of the U.S. Per Capita Market Income of $19,305 ($12,934 or lower) or 200% of poverty and one other indicator. (Per capita market income is per capita income less transfer payments.)

At the row variable prompt, *type* **83)PRES.VT92** and, at the column variable prompt, *enter* **87)DISTRSDCOL**. This last variable ranks counties from severely distressed to economically strong. *Write in* the **percentage** of counties supporting the Democrats in each of the four categories of the independent variable DISTRSDCOL:

Table 7.5 Counties going Democratic or Republican in the 1992 presidential election by economic status of county.

	Severely Distressed	Distressed	Middle	Strong Very Strong
Democratic				
Republican				

Do you see any trend here? Look across the rows. The more distressed the counties, the more they tend to favor the Democrats: 65 percent of the severely distressed counties support them, while 70 percent of the counties in strong (good economic) condition voted Republican.

Notice that the cell differences are mostly greater than 10 percent across the table. Researchers assume that differences greater than 10 percent are "significant." They also have a more precise way of testing for significance, called a "chi-square." *Press* Stat (for statistics) and you'll see that

Chi-square: 15.608   (Prob. = 0.000)

To repeat what has been discussed earlier (see the box on page 29), "Prob." stands for the probability of error in positing an association between two variables in a population. Probability is used to determine the chances of being wrong in claiming that a relationship found between variables in a *sample* will also be found in the *population from with the sample was drawn*. If we were working with a sample taken from all the counties in the United States, our chances of being wrong in asserting there is a relationship between party choice in the 1992 election and county economic status throughout the country is less than one in a thousand ($p < .001$). Those are good odds at any race track. But here we are not dealing with a *sample*, but the entire *population* of Appalachian counties, and therefore *the "p value" indicates the chances that our chi-quare (x^2) was a product of random factors*, rather than being an indication of association between variables. Still, the odds are a thousand to one supporting our assertion of a relationship between variables.

The probability score must be less than 0.05 (less than one chance in twenty) to indicate "significant" association between variables. The probability or "p value" is the first thing to look for to see if a statistical measure (such as x^2) is significant. If $p < .05$, you have significance; if $p > .05$ the results are not significant (written as "n.s.").

On the statistics screen below the chi-square and probability measures, you will see **V:0.199 C:0.195** and **Lambda (DV=83):0.146**. These "*chi-square based measures of association*" are indicators of the **strength** of the relationship between the two variables. "C" stands for Pearson's coefficient of contingency and "V" for Cramer's V. "Lambda" is Guttman's coefficient of predictability. You can learn more about these measures and how to compute them in a statistics course, but here you just need to know how to read them. (You don't have to be a mechanic to drive a car. You can use these indicators just the way you use your car without having to build your own engine first.) How do you interpret these numbers? Roughly, **a score under 0.10 suggests a weak relationship, scores between 0.10 and 0.30 are moderate and those higher than 0.30 are strong**. All three measures (C, V and Lambda) here suggest a moderate relationship between the counties' economic condition and party choice.

You have found two independent variables (subregion and county economic status) that affect voting patterns. Let's look for others. Does location of residence affect voting patterns? *Enter* **83** as the dependent, row variable and **6)CITY** as the independent variable. *Press* <ENTER> until the table appears and then *press* **C** to obtain column percentages:

What percentage of the nonmetropolitan counties supported the Democrats? _____

What percentage of the nonmetropolitan counties supported the Republicans? _____

What percentage of the metropolitan counties supported the Democrats? _____

What percentage of the metropolitan counties supported the Republicans? _____

Press **R** for row percentages.

What percentage of the Democratic supporters were nonmetropolitan? _____

What percentage of the Democratic supporters were metropolitan? _____

What percentage of the Republican supporters were nonmetropolitan? _____

What percentage of the Republican supporters were metropolitan? _____

Press **S** for statistics. x^2 (chi square) = _____ (prob. = 0.____)

C=0.____   V=0._____   Lambda (DV83)= 0.____

Was there a significant difference between urban and rural voters in the 1992 presidential election?

_____Yes   _____No   Check one and use your data to explain your choice below:

What about differences between counties in highland areas (over 1000 feet in altitude) and the rest of the region? *Enter 83* as the row variable and *5 (Highlands)* as the column variable. *Press* <ENTER> until the table appears and then *press* "C" to obtain column percentages. After comparing percentages, *press* "S" for statistics.

x^2= _____.   Prob. = _____

C=0.____   V=0._____   Lambda (DV83)= 0.____

Was there a significant difference between highland and non-highland voters in the 1992 presidential election? Use your data to explain your choice:

Did people in counties with higher mean per capita income vote Republican in 1992? Variable 86)PC%US92COL is the continuous variable 32)PCAP%US broken down into four categories: 1) 45-60% of the average U.S. per capita income in 1992; 2) 61-75%, 3)76-90% and 4)91-125%. Let's hypothesize that increasing per capita income means increasing percentage of counties favoring the Republican ticket. *Enter* **83**)PRES.VT92 as the row variable land **86**)PC%US92 as the column variable. When the table appears, *press C* for column percentages and record the results below:

Table 7.6 Counties going Republican or Democratic in the 1992 presidential election by percentage of average U.S. per capita income.

	45-60%	61-75%	76-90%	91-125%
Democratic	65.5			
Republican				

Do the percentages suggest a trend here? Describe it:

Even though we're dealing with population data and not a sample of a population, let's see if chi-square and chi-square based measures of association support our hypothesis:

$$\text{Chi-square } (x^{2)} = _____ \qquad (\text{Prob} = 0.006)$$

$$C=\underline{0.\_\_\_} \qquad V=\underline{0.\_\_\_\_\_} \qquad \text{Lambda (DV83)}= \underline{0.\_\_\_\_}$$

Can we accept or reject our hypothesis about a relationship between increasing affluence and voting Republican?

GOOD! You can now make and read **tables** and interpret **measures of association**. Remember what was said at the start of the chapter about using **tables for categorical variables** and **scatterplots and correlations for numerical ("interval/ratio") variables**. What kind of variable is 83)PRES.VT92? *Press* **F3**, *arrow down to* **83** *and press the right arrow* to see its three values: 1) DEMOCRATIC 2) REPUBLICAN 3) PEROT. These values represent three categories of this <u>categorical</u> variable. *Now use the up arrow to* 77) DEM.VOTE92, *press the right arrow and write its long label here:*

1992: _____

Notice that, instead of three categories, we have percentages: a range of thousands of possible scores ranging between 0 and 100 (0.01...26.58...65.21..etc). The data is *continuous*, not *categorical*. Each county potentially has a different score from every other county and thus, in a table, each county would demand a separate row. The table would have too many rows to be of any use. So, instead of the tables that work so well for categorical data, scatterplots, regressions and correlations are employed in the analysis of relationships between continuous variables. You have already seen this in Chapter V. Let's track some voting data using continuous variables. From the STATISTICAL ANALYSIS menu, *select* **F. Scatterplot.**

Let's see if the Democrats did better in areas where there was greater poverty: *Enter* 77)DEM.VOTE92 *as the dependent variable and* **39)%POOR 89** *as the independent variable. Press <ENTER> twice to bypass the subset request. When the scatterplot appears, press* Line, *write in the labels for the* X AXIS *and the* Y AXIS *and draw in the regression line:*

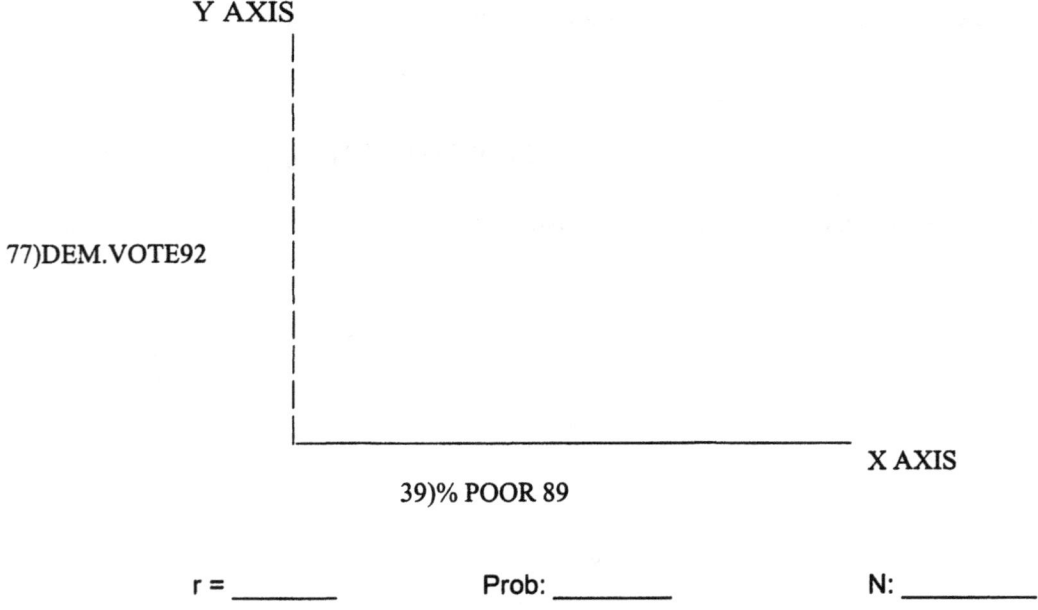

r = _____   Prob: _____   N: _____

To review methods for interpreting these results, refer back to the opening of Chapter V (pp53-54). *Describe the strength and direction (positive or negative)* of the relationship between percentage of poverty in a county and the percentage of votes for the Democrats:

Did the Democrats do better in counties having higher unemployment. *Enter* **77)DEM.VOTE92** as the dependent variable and **37)UNEMP 91** as the independent variable. *Press <ENTER> twice* to bypass the subset request. When the scatterplot appears, *press* Line and *write in the labels for the* X AXIS *and the* Y AXIS *and draw in* the regression line:

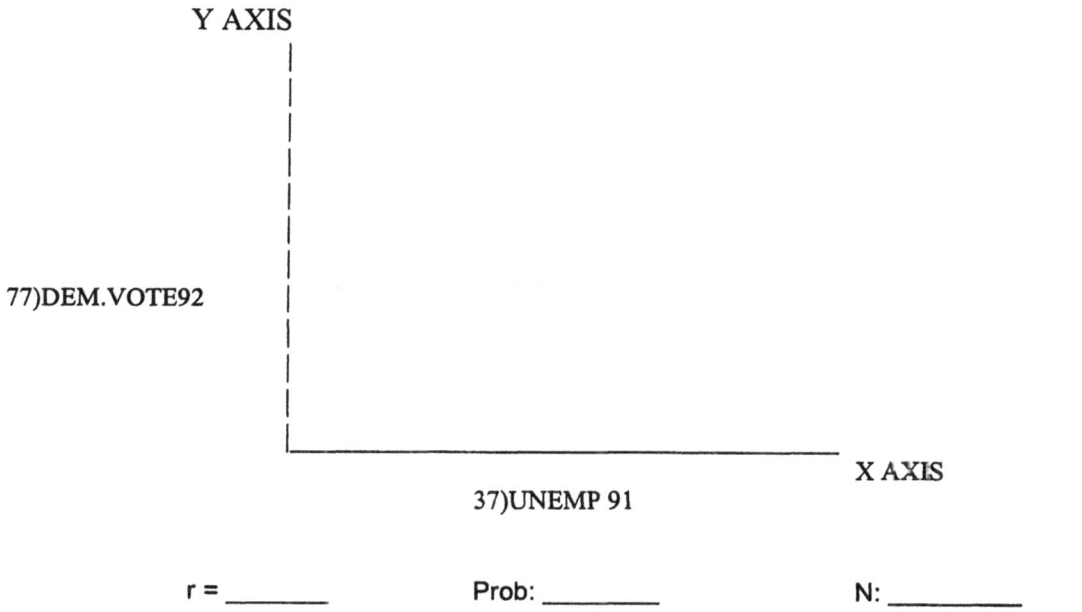

r = _____   Prob: _____   N: _____

Describe the strength and direction (positive or negative) of the relationship between unemployment and the percentage of votes in a county for the Democrats:

Hmm. I wonder if these results suggest that the higher a county's average per capita income, the higher the Republican vote. *Enter* **78)REP.VOTE92** as the dependent variable and **32)PERCAP 92** as the independent variable. *Press <ENTER> twice* to bypass the subset request. When the scatterplot appears, *press* **Line**, *write in the labels* and *draw in the regression line:*

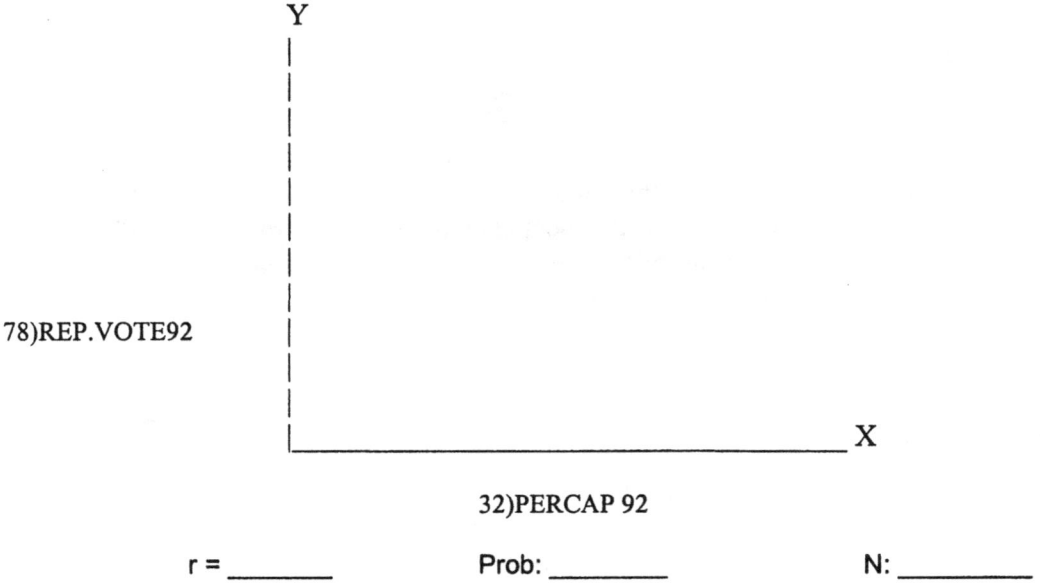

r = _____   Prob: _____   N: _____

Describe the strength and direction of the relationship between the counties' average 1992 per capita incomes and percentages of votes for the Republicans.

It looks like support for the Republicans was fairly steady across income levels. Might that have changed from the 1980 election? *Enter* **70)REP.VOTE80** as the dependent variable and **88)PERCAP$81** as the independent variable. *Press <ENTER> twice* to bypass the subset request. When the scatterplot appears, *press* Line and draw in the regression line:

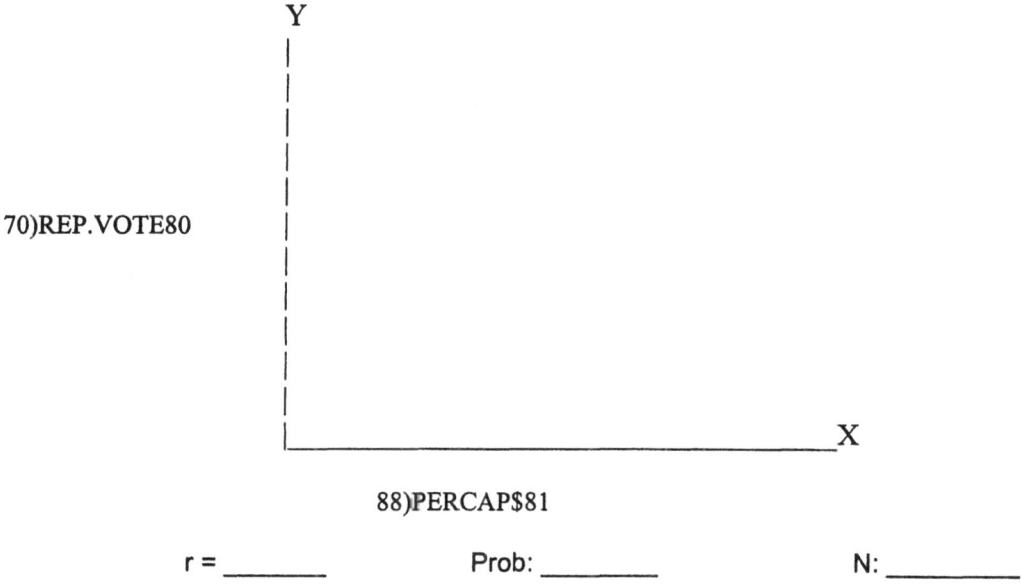

Describe the strength and direction of the relationship between the counties' average 1981 per capita incomes and percentages of votes for the Republicans.

Do you see any differences between the 1992 and the 1980 results?

HEY! WHAT ABOUT ROSS PEROT-THE INDEPENDENT PARTY CANDIDATE! WHAT CORRELATIONS CAN WE FIND WITH HIS CANDIDACY? DID THE POOR CITIZENS, DEPRIVED OF EDUCATIONAL AND ECONOMIC OPPORTUNITY AND THUS FED UP WITH "THE SYSTEM" OF THE TRADITIONAL PARTIES, THROW THEIR SUPPORT TO HIM? WAS IT A MATTER OF "RADICALS FOR ROSS?" *Enter* **79)**PER.VOTE92 as the dependent variable and **32)**PERCAP 92 as the independent variable. *Press <ENTER> twice* to bypass the subset request. When the scatterplot appears, *press* Line and draw in the regression line:

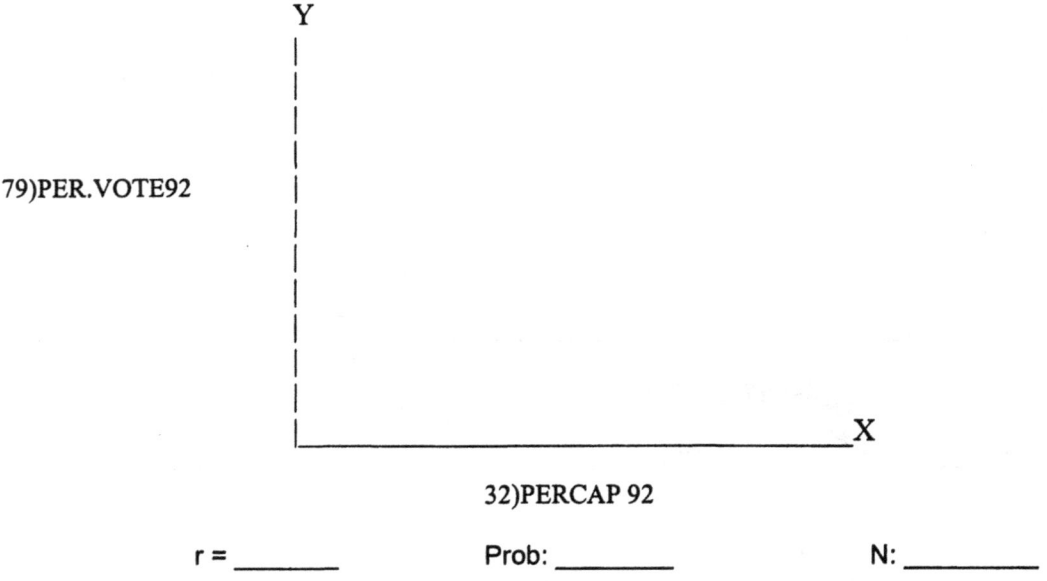

r = _____   Prob: _____   N: _____

Describe the strength and direction of the relationship between the counties' average 1992 per capita incomes and percentages of votes for Ross Perot:

What about support for Perot and levels of educational attainment? *Enter* **79)PER.VOTE92** as the dependent variable and **27)H.S.GRAD90** as the independent variable. *Press <ENTER> twice* to bypass the subset request. When the scatterplot appears, *press* Line and draw in the regression line:

Press X and enter the long label for 27)H.S.GRAD90:

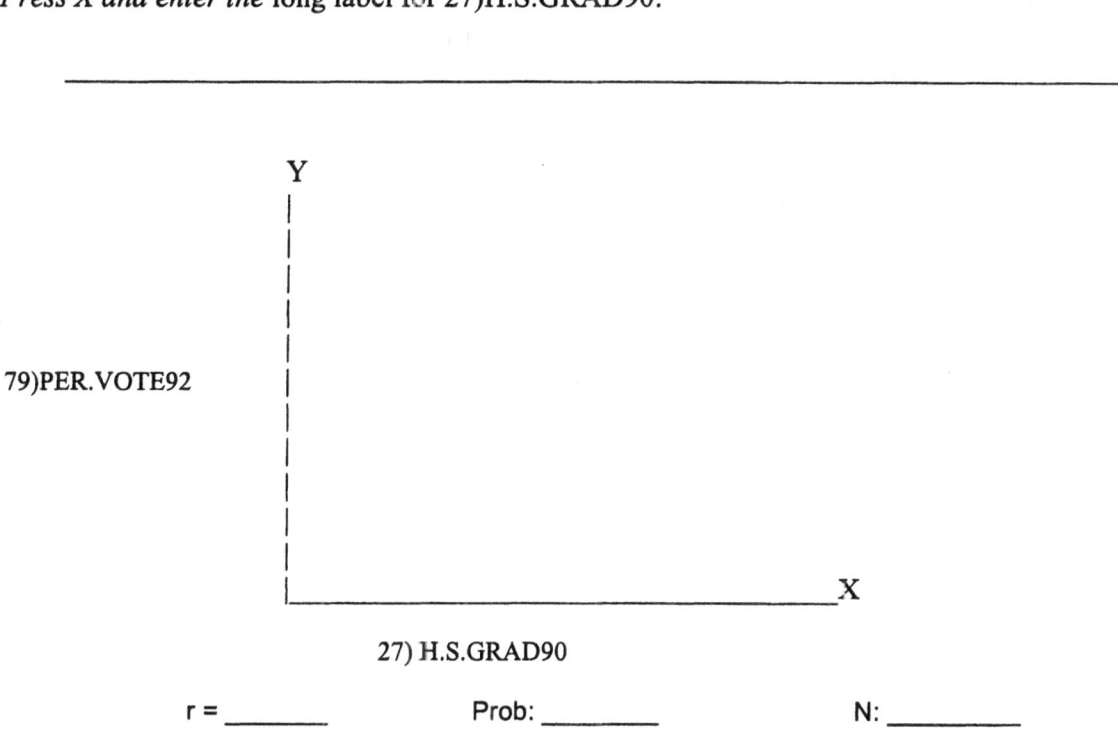

Describe the strength and direction of the relationship between the counties's average 1990 percent of people 25 and over who have a high school degree and the percentages of their votes cast for Ross Perot:

Summarize the results of the last two plots. Who voted for Perot, the Independent candidate?

Gee, Ross, that's pretty impressive. But with all those better off and better educated people supporting you, how come you didn't win?

Well, Tom, it doesn't take a rocket scientist to look at the percentages: *Return to the* DATA AND FILE MANAGEMENT menu and select **E. Codebook**. *Type* **1** and *press* <ENTER> to send the data to your monitor screen. You will be asked if you wish to stratify, which means break down one variable by another as you would in a table. The default setting is N, meaning no. *Press* <ENTER> to accept the default setting and again a second time to bypass the request for a subset. *Type* **79)PER.VOTE92** as the only variable to be listed. You'll see that the mean (average) percentage of votes for Perot in all the Appalachian counties was only 15 percent. Not a majority--not this time!

Try stratifying this variable by **3)THREE REGN** to see if voters in one of the three subregions might have been more favorable to Perot: *Press* <ENTER> to begin the codebook process again.

Type **1** and *press* <ENTER> to send the data to your monitor screen. *Type* **Y** at the "Do you wish to stratify?" prompt. *Type* **3** as the stratifying variable. *Press* <ENTER> to bypass the request for a subset and *enter* **79** as the only variable to be listed. List the results below:

REGION	N	Mean
North		
Central		
Southern		

Well, how about that for a candidate from Texas! He got about double the percentage of votes in the _____ subregion of Appalachia.

In this chapter, you have learned about:
    how to use quantitative methods in the analysis of voting behavior
    differences in voting behavior in different Appalachian subregions
    employing tables in data analysis
    the idea of probability
    chi-square (x^2) as a measure of the ability of a sample's findings to be generalized to a population
    differences between categorical and continuous variables
    labels for X and Y axes
    regression lines in scatterplots

Review your data and, as you have done previously, write a summary of your findings in this chapter. If you like, you can gather additional data by looking voting patterns by ethnic group, location, education and income level. Enjoy!

Another assignment possibility: Write a strategy for a presidential candidate touring the Appalachian region. What topics should she or he emphasize in different parts of the region?

VIII. Race and Region: Minorities in Appalachia

Multiple Regression

In Chapter III you saw that, contrary to the stereotype of an all-Anglo-Saxon Appalachia, the region is ethnically and culturally diverse, representing many nations and parts of the world. The question raised in this chapter is whether two of its ethnic groups, Native American and African American, enjoy the same opportunities and quality of life as other residents.

From the STATISTICAL ANALYSIS menu. *Select* **G. Correlation.** *Press F3* and use the down arrow to move down the list of variables and the left arrow to select those listed below. You want to see how the percentages of Native and African Americans (11:%AMER.IN90) and (18: %BLACK90) correlate with per capita income (32:PERCAP92), unemployment (37:UNEMP91), poverty (39:%POOR89); children in poverty (43:CHILD POR89); infant mortality (44: INFANT90-2); the number of physicians per 100,000 people (45: DR.RATE 90); the percentage of people over 25 with a high school degree (27: H.S. GRAD90), and the percentage of people with an Associate Degree or some college (30: COLLEGE90). Write the results below:

Table 6.1 Socio-Economic Indicators by Ethnic Group

	11)%AMER.IN90	18) %BLACK90
32) PERCAP 92		
37) UNEMP 91		
39) %POOR 89		
43) CHLD POR89		
44) INFANT 90-2		
45) DR.RATE90		
27) H.S. GRAD90		
30) COLLEGE 90		

List the labels of any correlation r that is greater than plus or minus 0.2:

_____   _____

Compare these results to the guide for explaining strength of association on page 46. Are there strong associations between ethnic group and opportunity? Describe what you see:

On the whole, discrimination IS/IS NOT (choose one) evident from these data. BUT, WAIT A MINUTE! Maybe discrimination differs in different parts of Appalachia. We know from chapter II (page 15) that counties in the Southern subregion tend to have higher percentages of African Americans than the North or Central subregions. We see just how much more by using the ANOVA function. From the STATISTICAL ANALYSIS menu select **C. Analysis of Variance**. At the dependent variable prompt, *type **18)**%BLACK90 and press <ENTER>*. At the independent variable prompt, *type **3)**Three Regn and press <ENTER>* twice to bypass the request for a subset variable. Notice the steep slope of the mean line on the plot. *Type* **M** (for mean) and enter the mean African American population for each of the three subregions. Repeat the same steps, but this time replace variable 18)%BLACK with **11)%AMER.IN90**.

Table 6.2 Ethnic Group by Subregion

Region	N (number of counties)	Mean (% BLACK90)	Mean (%AMER.IND)
North	144		
Central	84		
Southern	171		

Wow, that's quite a difference! On average, there are more than 6½ times as many African Americans and three times as many Native Americans in the Southern subregion's counties than there are in the North and Central areas. The Southern region historically has been the one associated with discrimination against non whites--but it's also more than 30 years after the Equal Opportunity and Voting Rights Acts and other legislation aimed at promoting equality. Maybe discrimination and economic inequality have been eliminated. Let's recreate the correlation matrix, but this time eliminate the 228 northern and central counties which may be concealing some important relationships and use the Southern subregion's 171 counties as a data subset.

From the STATISTICAL ANALYSIS menu, *select* **G. Correlation.** *Press* **F3** and use the left arrow to select the following variables: 11) %AMER.IN90, 18) %BLACK90); 32) PERCAP92; 37) UNEMP91; 39) %POOR 89, 43) CHILD POR89; 44) INFANT90-2; 45) DR.RATE90; 27) H.S. GRAD90) and 30) COLLEGE90. At the prompt for a subset *type* **3**. *Enter* **3** for the "lower limit" and **3** *again* for the upper limit. *Press <ENTER> twice* to bypass a second subset request and wait for the matrix to appear. Write in the results:

Table 6.3 Subset: Southern Appalachian Subregion

	11)%AMER.IN90	18) %BLACK90
32) PERCAP 92		
37) UNEMP 91		
39) %POOR 89		
43) CHLD POR89		
44) INFANT 90-2		
45) DR.RATE90		
27) H.S. GRAD90		
30) COLLEGE 90		

List the labels any correlation r that is greater than plus or minus 0.2 (which therefore has at least a moderate strength of association) and, in a simple sentence, explain the association between the two variables:

___

___

___

___

___

___

___

___

Since the percentages of Blacks in southern Appalachian counties are so much higher than those of Native Americans, let's focus our analysis on African Americans. Begin by comparing correlations found in all of Appalachia with those of the Southern subregion. Fill in the second column with data from Table 6.1 and the third column with the correlations found in Table 6.3

Table 6.4 Blacks in Appalachia and the Southern Subregion

	BLACKS IN ALL OF APPALACHIA	BLACKS IN SOUTHERN SUBREGION
32) PERCAP 92		
37) UNEMP 91		
39) %POOR 89		
43) CHLD POR89		
44) INFANT 90-2		
45) DR.RATE90		
27) H.S. GRAD90		
30) COLLEGE 90		

Describe the results of this table, row by row, taking special note of any large differences. Then summarize your findings.

_____

_____

_____

_____

_____

_____

Might these results be affected by location? Does living in Southern Appalachian *metropolitan* counties including or adjoining cities improve economic opportunities for African Americans? From the red STATISTICAL ANALYSIS menu. *Select* **G. Correlation**. *Press* **F3** and use the left arrow to select the following variables: 18) %BLACK90; 32) PERCAP 92; 37) UNEMP91; 39) %POOR89, 43) CHILD POR89; 44) INFANT90-2; 45) DR.RATE90; 27) H.S. GRAD90 and 30)COLLEGE90. At the prompt for a subset, *type* **3**. *Enter* **3** for the "lower limit" and **3** again for the upper limit. At the prompt for a second subset *type* **6**. *Enter* **1** for the "lower limit" and **1** *again* for the "upper limit." *Press* *<ENTER>* *twice* to bypass a third subset request and wait for the matrix to appear. Record the results in the second column of Table 6.5. Enter data from the previous table's (Table 6.4) third column in the third column here:

Table 6.5 Blacks in the Southern Subregion & Southern Metro Areas

	BLACKS IN SOUTHERN SUBREGION METRO AREAS	BLACKS IN SOUTHERN SUBREGION (from Table 6.4)
32) PERCAP 92		
37) UNEMP 91		
39) %POOR 89		
43) CHLD POR89		
44) INFANT 90-2		
45) DR.RATE90		
27) H.S. GRAD90		
30) COLLEGE 90		

Compare the results across the rows (for example the difference in the correlations for per capita income in 1) metro areas as against 2) the entire Southern subregion.

___

___

___

___

___

A statistical method called **multiple regression** provides another way to explore the impacts of discrimination. Multiple regression allows the researcher to explore the **combined effects** of two or more independent variables on a dependent variable, for example the impacts of being rural and being Black on being poor. Let's see how several variables related to poverty correlate. From the **STATISTICAL ANALYSIS** menu, *select* **G. Correlation** and enter the following variables: 8)%RURAL90, 18)%BLACK90, 37)UNEMP91, 39)%POOR 89, and 47)F HEAD/C90 (1990: percent of households that are female headed with own children with no spouse present). When asked for a subset *enter* **3** as the variable and **3** again for both the lower and upper limits. You should get a correlation matrix for the 171 counties found in the southern region. *Enter the results* from the column headed by <u>39)% Poor 89</u>:

Table 6.6

	39) %POOR 89
8)%RURAL90	
18)%BLACK90	
37)UNEMP 91	
47)F HEAD/C90	

There are some very strong correlations here (so strong we run the risk of a statistical problem called "multicollinarity" where the independent variables correlate too highly). We need to eliminate the overlap between independent variables (a lot of Blacks live in rural areas and are unemployed) as they affect the dependent variable 39)%POOR 89 to find out which of the independent variables have the most impact on poverty.

From the **STATISTICAL ANALYSIS** menu, *select* **I. Regression** and *enter* **39)%POOR 89** as the dependent variable. For the independent variables, *type* **8) %RURAL90, 18) %BLACK90,** and **37)UNEMP 91**. Focus on the <u>Southern subregion</u> by *entering* **3** at the request for a subset and *typing* **3** for both the low and high values. You should see:

Figure 6.1

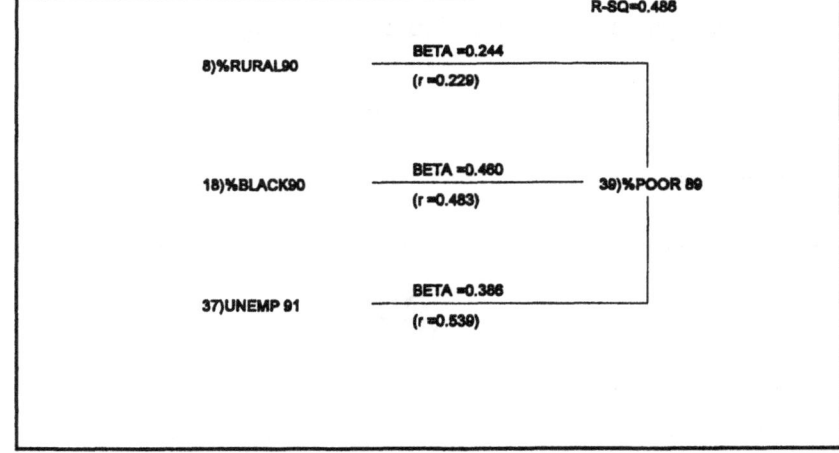

106

Notice the R-SQ (R^2) in the upper right hand corner. It is a measure of the combined effects of the three independent variables on the dependent variable %POOR. Put another way, 48.6% of the variance or difference in poverty rates among the 171 southern counties is **explained** by these three variables. The correlation coefficients "r", that you wrote into the table on the previous page are listed below the line linking each independent variable to the dependent variable %POOR. Above the same line is a new measure called a BETA. This is a **standardized beta**, indicating how much the dependent variable would change with a change of one standard deviation in the independent variable, if the effects of the other independent variables were removed. For example, with the effects of %RURAL and UNEMPLOYMENT removed, we would predict that an increase of one standard deviation of %BLACK would result in .460 increase in poverty. Since this is the highest beta in the graph, it would appear that discrimination against Blacks in these Southern counties is a primary cause of their impoverishment.

WAIT A MINUTE! MAYBE RACE ISN'T THE ISSUE. WHAT ABOUT THE STATE OF THE FAMILY AND POVERTY? IN TABLE 6.6, THE CORRELATION BETWEEN % FEMALE HEADS OF HOUSEHOLDS WITH CHILDREN AND % BLACK WAS VERY STRONG (.844) AS IT WAS WITH POVERTY (.505). MAYBE THE HIGH BETA SCORE FOR %BLACK IS **SPURIOUS** (NOT REAL), MASKING A **GENUINE** CAUSAL RELATIONSHIP BETWEEN FAMILY STRUCTURE AND POVERTY.

Put another way, the correlation between %Black and poverty suggests the following causal relationship:

11)%BLACK 90 --------------> 39)%POOR 89

But maybe the situation is:

11)%BLACK ----------> 47)F HEAD/C90 ------------> 39)%POOR

Is 47)F HEAD/C90 an **intervening** variable and a genuine cause of poverty? Let's see: Select **I. Regression** and *enter* 39) %POOR as the dependent variable. For the independent variables, *type* **8)** %RURAL 90, **18)** %BLACK90, **37)** UNEMP 91 and this time *add* **47)** F HEAD/C90. Focus on the Southern subregion by *entering* **3** at the request for a subset and *typing* **3** for both the low and high values.

107

Figure 6.2

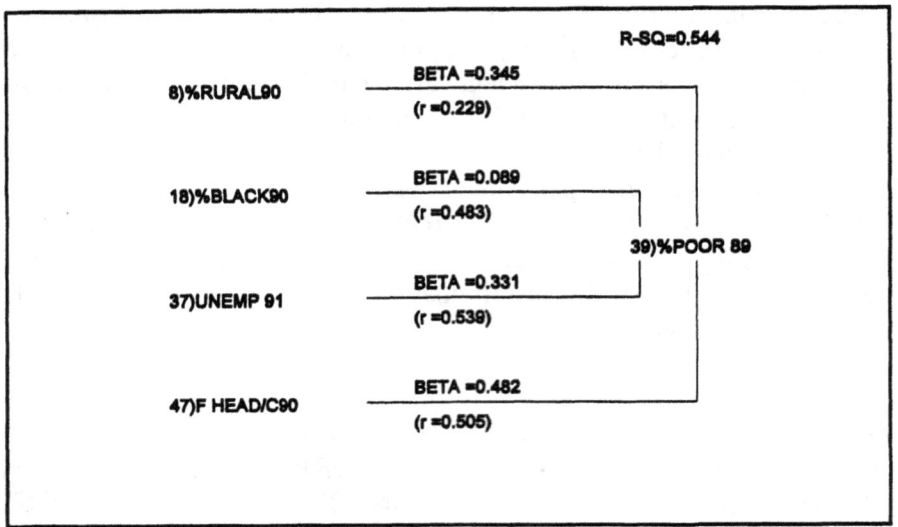

The R-SQ has been bumped up from 0.486 to 0.544: our ability to explain changes in the poverty rate has increased. Furthermore, the relationship between percentage of black people in a county and poverty now appears to be **spurious**, the *beta* having dropped from 0.460 to 0.089. The percentage of female heads of households with children and no husband present appears to be the most powerful independent variable affecting poverty. To repeat the language used here: the correlation between %Black and %Poor appears to be **spurious**; the correlation between female heads of households with children and poverty seems **genuine**.

This is a very controversial finding. How do you explain it? Is single parenting a matter of choice, culture or a product of historical and social conditions? Most single parents are women. Is this an indication of discrimination against women in wage and salary structures? Is this an indication of less buying power for wage earners in general--do more households need the buying power of two wage earners than was the case ten, twenty or thirty years ago? Maybe the relationship is something like

11)%BLACK --->47)F HEAD/C90 --->WOMENS' JOBS/WAGE LEVELS--->39)%POOR

Quantitative analysis often raises more questions than it answers, sending us on a search for more data. Let's continue our inquiry with the data we have at hand by conducting a multiple regression for the entire Appalachian region: Select **I. Regression** and *enter* **39)** %POOR as the dependent variable. For the independent variables, *type* **8)**%RURAL 90, **18)** %BLACK90, **37)**UNEMP91 and **47)**F HEAD/C90. *DON'T select a subset* this time to obtain results for all 399 Appalachian counties.

How much of the variance in the dependent variable can be explained by the independent variables? In other words, R^2 = _____ .

Write the BETAs into the following graph

Figure 6.3

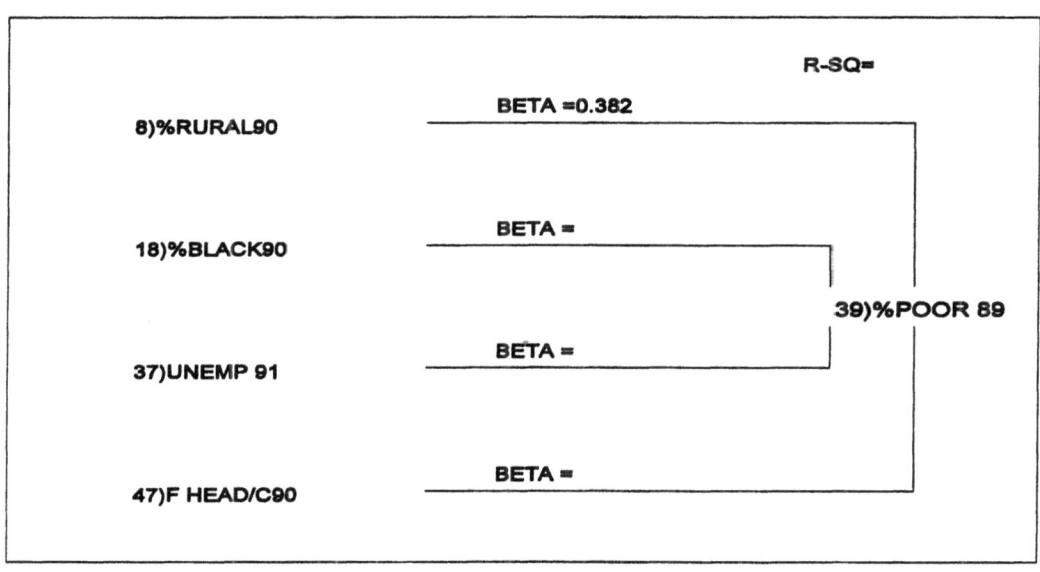

Describe your results, taking special note of the change in 18)%BLACK90 caused by the addition of 48)%F HEAD/C90 as an additional independent variable. Compare the results for the entire Appalachian region to those for the Southern subregion. Is there a difference or are they pretty much the same?

Let's see if there is a similar pattern for Native Americans living in the Southern *subregion: Select* **I. Regression** and *enter* 39) %POOR as the dependent variable. For the independent variables, *type* **8)%RURAL 90, 11)%AMER.IN90, 37)UNEMP91** and this time add **47)F HEAD/C90**. Again, *choose the Southern subset (3/3/3)*. You should get the following results:

Figure 6.4

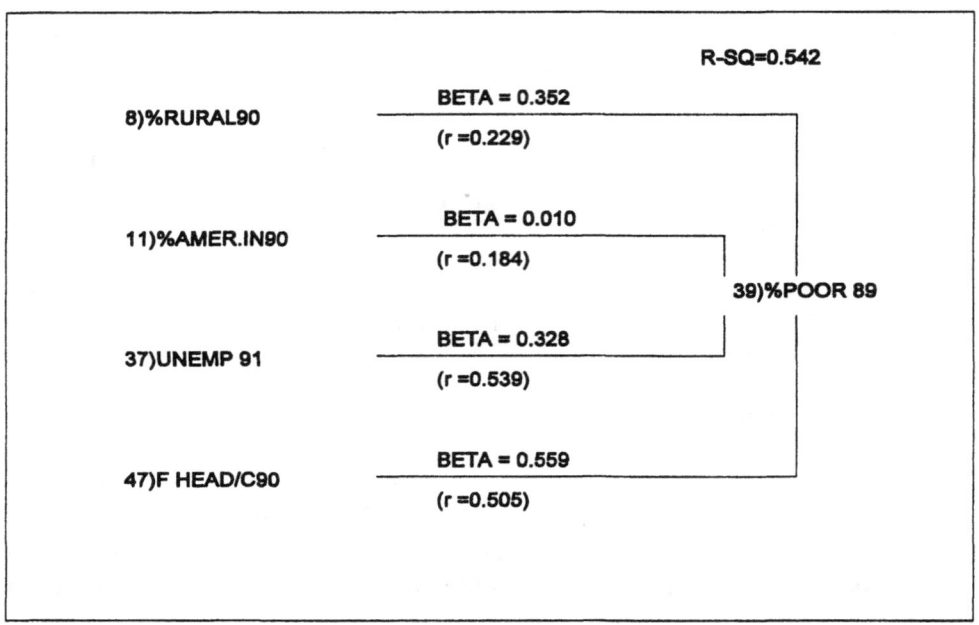

Which independent variable has the <u>strongest</u> association with poverty?

_____

_____

Which independent variable has the <u>weakest</u> association with poverty?

_____

_____

Reviewing the data, do you think race is the most salient cause, or might it be location (urban or rural) and/or the kind of household structure?

_____

_____

What about other ethnic groups? Does the nature of the household and location maintain their strong *betas* when dealing with "non-minority" Caucasian groups such as those claiming English and German ancestry? Look at the following graph carefully:

Figure 6.5

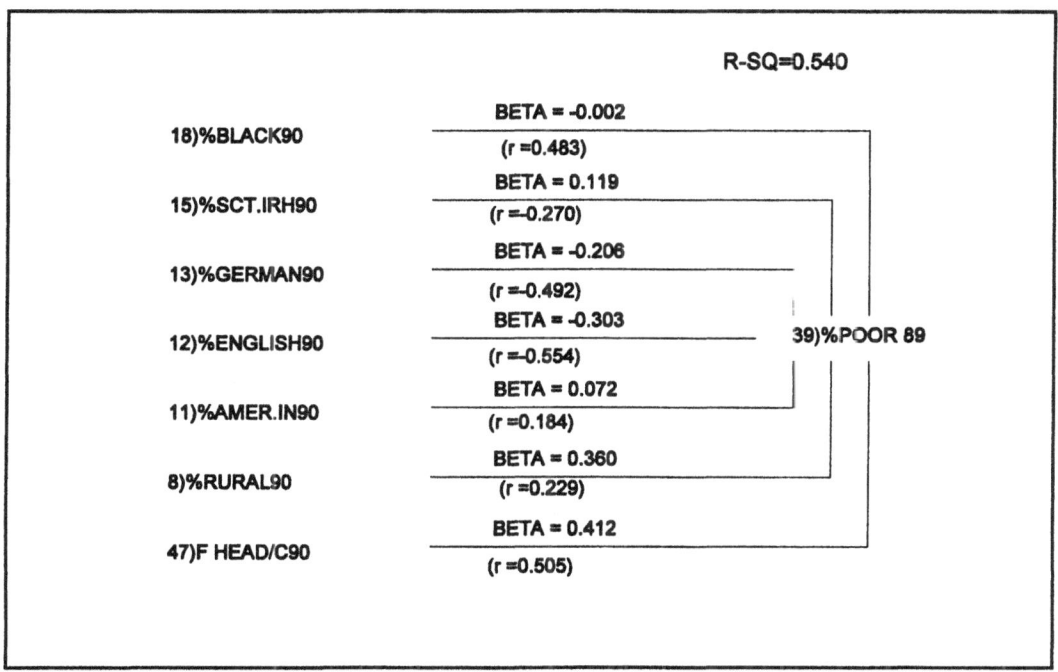

Remember that the independent variables' *betas* are above the lines. Note that the correlations for Native and African Americans are reduced to insignificance by the multiple regression procedure. People claiming Scotch-Irish descent have a weak, positive *beta*, while those claiming German and English descent have weak-to-moderate negative *betas*. Location and household type still have the highest *beta* scores.

What about educational opportunity and location? At the dependent variable prompt, *enter* **30)COLLEGE 90**. For independent variables, *enter* **8)%RURAL** and **18)%BLACK**. Describe your results: Is location or race the more serious barrier to attending college?

In this chapter, you have examined some of the circumstances affecting the life chances of Native Americans and especially African Americans living in Appalachia. You have employed correlation coefficients and multiple regression techniques in your data analysis. You should know the meaning of r, *beta* and R^2. Using the F3 function key, you can explore correlations and multiple regressions between other variables. Relate your findings to Susan Emley Keefe and William Turner's discussions of African Americans as "a racial minority within a cultural minority," who suffer greater deprivation than Blacks elsewhere in the United States (Keefe, 1998, 150; Turner and Cabbell, 1985, xix).

Review the data and summarize your findings. What have you learned about the impact of discrimination, location, and wage structures on life chances? What questions have the data *not* answered and what new questions have been raised? Conclude your report with suggestions for future research.

Defining Appalachia

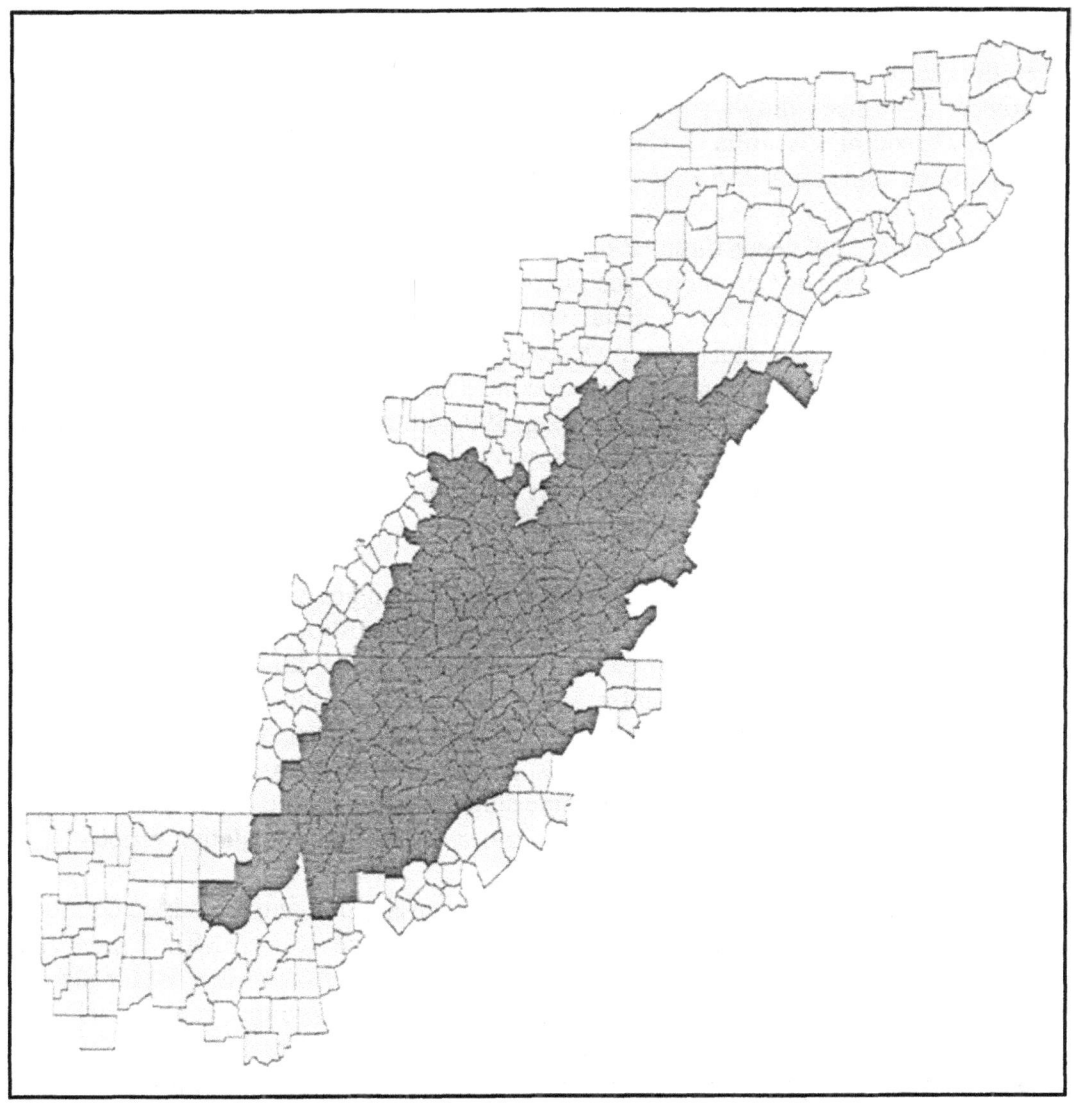

The darker portion of the map marks 179 counties in seven states that both the 1962 Ford study and the U.S. Congress included in their definitions of the Appalachian region. The lighter portion indicates the counties added in the legislative process surrounding the passage of the Appalachian Redevelopment Act of 1965 (which excluded 10 of Ford's counties in the Virginian Blue Ridge). Ford's definition followed a description of "state economic areas," developed in 1950 by the Bureau of the Census and the U.S. Department of Agriculture, in which counties having a similar economic base where grouped together. In the following analysis, the darker area is defined as the "core counties" of the Appalachian region. The surrounding 220 counties, labeled "added counties," combine with the core to make the larger region of 399 counties in 13 states.

IX. A Region with Many Definitions

Appalachia has been defined in terms of student perceptions, historical and geological characteristics, unique cultural folkways, economy and problems. One observer recently noted that the boundaries have been drawn so many times that there can be no "correct" definition of the region. In 1921, sociologist John C. Campbell described Appalachia as a unique cultural area in the United States including *256 counties in nine states*: Maryland, Virginia, West Virginia, Kentucky, Tennessee, North and South Carolina, Georgia and Alabama. In 1962, a study of the region's social-economic needs directed by Thomas R. Ford at the University of Kentucky, used a 1950s U.S. Department of Commerce designation of *189 counties in seven states* (Maryland and South Carolina were excluded). The Appalachian Redevelopment Act of 1965 created a federally-designated region based on a definition by state governors and representatives in Congress. This new region was to include *397 (now 406) counties in 13 states*. When the database for this book was created in 1996, the region was defined as having 399 counties. The four new states added by the Congress to the Ford and Campbell lists were New York, Pennsylvania, Ohio and Mississippi. (For an Internet map showing different definitions of the region go to http://www.unc.edu/~whisnant/appal/maps/Appreg.gif.)

Weak economies were cited as the primary reason for including new counties (nearly doubling the number of counties) in this new region, which would receive millions of dollars in federal aid. Did politics explode the size of the region? The more states included, the more votes and chances of passage of an Appalachian development program in Congress. But, if Congress was concerned about alleviating poverty and economic distress, should it have targeted its funds on the smaller area previously cited earlier by regional experts, or did it do the right thing by virtually doubling the size of Appalachia from 179 counties in nine states to 399 counties in 13 states? With almost 40 years of hindsight, we can reflect upon the wisdom of the 1965 legislative process.

To begin our analysis, let's get a bird's eye view of the core region and the added counties. *Select* **I. Open, Look, Erase or Copy File** from the DATA AND FILE MANAGEMENT menu. Highlight the APCOUNTY file and *press <ENTER>*. Switch to the STATISTICAL ANALYSIS menu and *select* **E. Mapping Variables**. At the "variable to be mapped" prompt, *type* **4**. When the map appears, you'll see that all of New York, Pennsylvania, Ohio and Mississippi are excluded from the core area as well as most of Alabama and portions of Georgia, South Carolina and North Carolina.

Now look at the overall region in terms of economic strength. The comparative economic positions of Appalachian counties can be found in two variables: The first is 36) DISTRESSED, where counties were ranked in 1988 on a five-point scale from "severely distressed" to "very strong" economies. I collapsed the two highest values "strong" and "very strong" together in variable 87) DISTRSDCOL, because there were only four "very strong" counties in the region (about 1%). *Make a map* of 87)DISTRSDCOL. *Press* Legend for clarification of the color coding.

Where do the counties in economic difficulty seem to be clustered? _____

_____

_____

Where are the relatively few (21) economically strong/very strong counties? _____

_____

_____

_____

For comparative rankings of the counties, *select* **A. Univariate Statistics**. At the prompt for the variable, *enter* 87, *press* <ENTER> *twice* to bypass the subset and you will see a pie chart showing the percentages of counties falling into one of the four categories. *Press* **B** (for Bar chart). You will see a large green arrow under the first bar, which is identified in the lower left section of the screen as "1) Severely Dis(tressed)," with a frequency of 89 counties, which make up 22.3% of the regions' 399 counties. Use the right arrow key to move to the second category, "Distressed," which has 50 counties or 12.5 percent. *Press* Table) and you'll see that the cumulative percentage for severely distressed and distressed counties is 34.8 percent.

Press <ENTER> to return to the variable prompt and again, *type* 87. At the subset prompt, *enter* 4)Appal Core and *select* 2 (Core County) as both the lower and upper limit. *Press* <ENTER> to bypass the second subset request. After the pie chart appears, *press* **B** for the bar chart. Notice the difference? What is the percentage of 1) severely distressed counties now? _____ What is the percentage of 2) distressed counties? _____ We have eliminated the "added counties," tacked onto Appalachia by the Congressional legislative process in 1964-65. *Press* Table and record the cumulative percentage for severely distressed and distressed counties: _____.

Hmm. It seems that about a third of the larger, 399-county Appalachia has economically distressed counties---but nearly one half of the 179 counties in the smaller, core region are in trouble. Let's make some bivariate tables to compare these 179 counties to the other 220 counties tacked on in the 1965 legislative process. From the STATISTICAL ANALYSIS menu, *select* **B. Tabular Statistics**. For the row (or dependent) variable, enter **87)DISTRSDCOL**. For the column (or independent) variable, *enter* **4)APAL CORE**. *Press* <ENTER> *three times* to obtain a table of the counties ranked by economic strength, but broken down into the two "core" and "added" regions. *Press* **C** for column percentages. The results should match table 8.1

Table 8.1. Percentage Appalachian Counties by Economic Status and Subregion

Economic Status	Added Counties	Core Counties	TOTAL
SEVERELY DISTRESSED	15.9%	30.2%	22.3%
DISTRESSED	9.5%	16.2%	12.5%
MIDDLE	67.7%	50.3%	59.9%
STRONG/VERY STRONG	6.8%	3.4%	4.3%
	100.0%	100.0%	100.0%

List the percentage of <u>severely distressed</u> counties in the two categories:

        Core counties   _____

        Added counties   _____

List the <u>cumulative</u> percentage of <u>severely distressed</u> and <u>distressed</u> counties in the two categories:

        Core counties   _____

        Added counties   _____

Are the two regions in similar economic condition? If not, how are they different?

_____

_____

_____

_____

_____

Incidentally, the core region has _____counties, while the added region has _____counties.

In 1995, the Appalachian Regional Commission again divided the regions counties into two categories: distressed and not distressed. (See the box on page 78 for definitions of "distressed"). Return to the STATISTICAL ANALYSIS menu and *select* **B. Tabular Statistics**. *Enter* **90** as the row variable and **4** as the column variable. *Label* the table and *write in* the <u>percentages</u>:

Table 8.2. _____

Economic Condition	Added Counties	Core Counties
Distressed		
Not distressed		
Total		

The data for 1999 Distressed Counties are found in variable 91. *Enter* **91** as the row variable and, again, **4** as the column variable and record the percentages:

Table 8.3. _____

Economic Condition	Added Counties	Core Counties
Distressed		
Not distressed		
Total		

Review the data from Tables 8.1, 8.2 and 8.3. Did the economic situation in the core counties improve between 1988 and 1999?

_____

_____

_____

_____

_____

Do people in the two regions make the same amount of money? Table 2 breaks mean (average) incomes down by core and added counties. Use the codebook function to make some comparisons:

From the DATA FILE AND MANAGEMENT menu *select* **E. Codebook.** *Select* **1** to send your results to the monitor screen. *Enter* **Y** (for yes) at the "Do you wish to stratify?" query. *Enter* **4)APPAL CORE** as the stratifying variable and *press <ENTER>* to bypass the subset request. *Type* **32,33,35** as the "list of variables to be included" and *press <ENTER>* to obtain the first of three tables: (Convert the numbers in the table to rounded-off dollars–for example, $15,109.)

Table 8.4: 1992 Counties' mean per capita income by Core and Added Counties

	N	Mean $
Added Counties	220	15,109
Core Counties	179	13,899

Subtract the core region's mean income from the "added county" category. The average income in the core region in 1992 was $_____ less than the average income of the counties added to the core by Congress in 1965. *Press <ENTER>* to obtain the second table of incomes, calculated as a percent of the U.S. average. *Fill in the cells for 1992 below. Press <ENTER>* again to obtain the third table and *fill in the cells* for 1970.

Table 8.5. Incomes *as a percentage* of the U.S. national average for 1970 and 1992.

	1970 Mean %	1992 Mean %
Added Counties		
Core Counties		

There seems to be a difference between the two categories of counties. In 1992, people in the Appalachian "core" counties made _____ percent of the national average per capita income, _____ percent less than people in the counties added to the region by the Congress in 1965 (whose average was _____ percent). Was there a similar gap 30 years ago when the ARC was founded? What does the table tell you?

_____

_____

_____

Let's examine the differences between the two (core, added) subregions, using **B. Tabular Statistics** in the STATISTICAL ANALYSIS menu. The *continuous* variable 33)PCAP%US92 is a comparison of each county's average income with the national average. If a county per capita income scored 100% of the U.S. average, it would be the same as the U.S. average. If it scored 125%, it would be 25% higher than the national average. If it scored 50%, its average (mean) income would be half of the U.S. average. Here, 33)PCAP%US92 has been *collapsed* into a *categorical* variable: 86) PC%US92COL. *Press* **F3**, *press* the "End" function key to get to the bottom of the variable list, *arrow up* to *highlight* **86** and *press* the right arrow key to see the category labels. The poorest counties, where per capita incomes range from 45 to 60 percent of the U.S. national average, are coded as 1. Per capita incomes between 61-75 percent of the national average are coded as 2; 76-90%=3 and 96-125%= 4.

At the prompt for a row variable, *enter* **86**. *Type* **4** for the column variable and *press* *<ENTER>* *twice*. *Press* "C" for column percentages and *enter* them here:

Table 8.6. Percentage of US mean per capita income of Appalachian counties by percentage core and added subregions.

Percentage of US Mean	Added Counties (percent)	Core Counties (percent)
1 45-60%		
2 61-75%		
3 76-90%		
4 91-125%		
Total %	100	100

It appears that the "core" subregion's percentage of counties in the poorest (45-60%) category is _____ percent higher than the added counties! As you did in chapter 4 (see page 35), compute this by using the formula below and multiplying the resulting ratio by 100 to convert it into a percentage.

<u>Core County - Added County</u>
Added County

Now it's your turn to see if there are other characteristics that distinguish these two Appalachian subregions from each other: Does the core region have a higher dropout rate than the 220 other counties? *Choose* **C. Analysis of Variance** to compare mean (average) dropout rates. *Press* **F3** to get a list of the 90 variables in this data file. *Press* **S** for search, and *type in* **HS** and you'll find that NOT N HS90 is variable 26. Press the right arrow and you will see the variable described. Write down that description here:

_____

Press <ENTER> to make the variable label disappear from the screen. You then can *mark* **26** with the left arrow and *press <ENTER>* twice so that "26 " appears as the response to the request for a dependent variable. *Type* **4**)APPAL CORE as the independent variable, *press <ENTER>* twice to bypass the subset request and obtain your graph. *Press* **M** to obtain the means and *write in* a title for the table together with the results:

Table 8.7 _____

Subregion	Mean % Not in High School
Added Counties	
Core Counties	

Using the formula on the previous page, it appears that the "core" subregion's mean percentage of people not in high school is _____ percent higher than the added counties.

Is there a difference in the two regions' unemployment rates? *Type* **37** (the 1991 county unemployment rates) as the dependent variable and, again, *enter* **4** as the independent variable. *Press <ENTER>* twice to bypass the subset request, review the graph, *press* **M** to obtain the means and *write in* the title and column labels along with the results:

Table 8.8 _____

_____	_____
Added Counties	
Core Counties	

It appears that the "core" counties' unemployment rate is _____% higher than the added counties.

Compare the poverty rates in the two regions. *Enter* **39** as the dependent variable and **4** as the independent variable. When you see the graph, *press* **Y** and write down the "long label" of the dependent variable here:

_____

Press **M** to obtain the means and write in the results:

Table 8.9. Mean poverty rates in core and added counties

Subregion	Poverty Rate
Added Counties	
Core Counties	

It appears that the core counties' poverty rate is _____ percent higher than the added counties.

What about the percentage of elderly people over 65 living in poverty? *Enter* **40** as the dependent variable and **4** as the independent variable. List the "long label" for the dependent variable:

_____

Enter the results below:

Table 8.10. Mean percentage of people over 65 below poverty level

Subregion	Poverty Rate >65
Added Counties	
Core Counties	

It appears that the core counties' poverty rate for people over 65 is _____ percent higher than the added counties.

What about children? *Enter* **43** as the dependent variable and **4** for the independent variable. Which region has the greater percentage of kids living below the poverty line?

Enter the results below:

Table 8.11. Mean percentage of children below poverty

Subregion	Children in Poverty
Added Counties	
Core Counties	

It appears that the core counties' poverty rate for children under 18 is _____ % higher than the added counties.

What about medical services? Which region has the most doctors? *Enter* **45** as the dependent variable and **4** as the independent variable. Write out the "long label" for 45 (*press* **Y** on the graph):

_____

Enter the results below:

Table 8.12. Nonfederal physicians per 100,000

Subregion	Physician rate
Added Counties	
Core Counties	

It appears that the core counties' number of physicians per 100,000 people is _____% *lower* than physician rate found in the added counties.

Which region received more federal assistance in 1990? *Enter* **68)FED$/CAP90** as the dependent variable and **4** for the independent variable.

Enter the results below:

Table 8.13. Direct Federal Expenditures and Grants Per Capita

Subregion	Expenditures & Grants (Rounded off in dollars)
Added Counties	
Core Counties	

Surprised? The core counties received _____ more federal assistance on a per capita basis than did the added counties. Might this be related to the Appalachian Regional Commission's Distressed Counties Program? Hmm. You're going to have to compare the means of Expenditures and Grants by Distressed Counties. *Enter* **68)FED$/CAP90** as the dependent variable and **91** for the independent variable.

Enter the results below:

Table 8.14. Direct Federal Expenditures and Grants Per Capita by Economic Status

Economic Status	Expenditures & Grants (Rounded off in dollars)
Distressed	
Not Distressed	

On average, the Distressed Counties received $_____ more than the other counties.

Stated another way, the Distressed Counties received _____ percent more in Federal funds than the other counties.

Students interested in public policy formation may want to research the *legislative process* involved in the passage of the Appalachian Redevelopment Act of 1965. Was there a connection between the number of votes needed in the House and Senate to get the bill through Congress and the mandated definition of the region? Consider the following data from the Congressional Quarterly summary of the 1965 first session of the 89th Congress (Volume XXI, pages 34-37):

Table 8.15. Numbers of Representatives from Appalachian States - 89th Congress (1965)

Core States		Added ARC States	
Alabama	8	Mississippi	5
Georgia	10	New York	41
Kentucky	7	Ohio	24
Maryland	8	Pennsylvania	27
North Carolina	11	TOTAL	97
South Carolina	6		
Tennessee	9		
Virginia	10		
West Virginia	5		
TOTAL	74		

Total from Appalachian Redevelopment Act States	171
Total in House of Representatives during 89th Congress	435

You can read about the legislative process surrounding the creation of the Appalachian Regional Commission and its region in the same CQ volume, pages 788-797.

Now consider the question asked at the outset of this chapter: Did the Congress act appropriately in defining the region as 399 counties in 13 states, or should it have focused on the smaller, "core" counties that both the United States Congress and the Ford study both considered part of the Appalachian region? As you have done at the conclusion of previous chapters, use the data you have generated in this one to develop and explain your argument. Be comparative. Be specific.

X. The Internet: Finding New Data in The Information Age

The data in the preceding chapters is already outdated! Computers have tremendously increased the capacity for data gathering and analysis, making new and revised information available on a continuous basis. How can you stay current? One source is the Internet, where you can find data at national, regional, state and county levels. You can access a website *directly*, if you know the URL (Universal Resource Locator). For example, the Appalachian Regional Commission's URL is http://www.arc.gov. You can access sites *indirectly* through "search engines" such as Yahoo or Google.

Try the direct approach first: see if you can find the latest Appalachian Regional Commission data on Distressed Counties. You'll need a *browser*, such Netscape or Explorer. In the "location" (URL) window at the top of your browser screen, *enter* "arc.gov."

Welcome to the Commission's home page. You will see half a dozen icons: About ARC; News, Events and Publications, etc. Each icon links to other pages. Use your mouse to *click on* Regional Research and Reports. *Click again on* Income Rates in Appalachia, (most recent year recorded). Toward the bottom of the page you will see a list of states in the Appalachian region. Click on any state for the latest county-by-county data in that state. This is the URL I used to update the data file for this edition of the book.

    What is the latest per capita income for the state of Alabama? _____

    What year is this data for? _____

    What is the latest per capita income for Bibb County, Alabama? _____

Click on the "back" button on your browser to return to the Regional Research page and select "Population Change in Appalachia, 1990–1999," (or whatever the most recent year given).

    Which state gained the most population between 1990 and 199(9)? _____

    Which state lost population in the same period? _____. Hmm. You surprised me!

Write in the data for the following counties:

	Population 1999	Percent gain/loss 1990-1999
Gwinnett, Georgia	_____	_____
Broome, New York	_____	_____
Henderson, North Carolina	_____	_____
Harlan, Kentucky	_____	_____

Return to the ARC home page and click on the "Site Index" at the bottom of the page. You can see from the list of topics that you have plenty of information to write a history of the organization. Of course, this history would be from the agency's perspective, so you would need to balance your research with other points of view. You'll need other URLs–those of colleges and universities, think tanks and advocacy groups. This is where the *indirect* method of Internet access is helpful. In your browser's "location" (URL) window at the top of your screen *enter* "Google.com." Just enter a topic–any topic–and you will be given a number of sites related to your key word. For your research here, *enter* "Appalachia" as the subject.

How many URLs did you find? _____ .

Find any college or university sites?   Yes   No   (circle one)

If yes, what is their connection to Appalachia? _____

_____

_____

_____

Find any advocacy groups?   Yes   No   (circle one)

If yes, what were their concerns about Appalachia? _____

_____

_____

_____

Find anything about Appalachian music?   Yes   No

How about Appalachian geology?   Yes   No

Type "Yahoo" in the location window at the top of your screen. When the Yahoo search engine appears on your screen, *enter* "Appalachia" in the search window. Some of the sites here will be those found in your Google search, but you will also find some new ones. How many categories _____ and how many sites _____ did Yahoo find for Appalachia?

Type "Alta Vista" in the location window at the top of your screen and you'll be taken to yet another search engine. Again, *enter* "Appalachia" in the search window.

How many web pages did Alta Vista find for you? _____

When you use search engines, you are likely to find new sites for whatever you are researching. As you found with Alta Vista, the amount of the information sometimes can be overwhelming. You can get lost in it. The direct access method (knowing the URL you need and accessing it) saves time.

Use the direct method to access another government agency, the Census Bureau. In the location window, *enter "http://www.census.gov."*

What is today's estimated population for the United States? _____

What is today's estimated population for the world? _____

Under the "PEOPLE" category you will find information on the following subjects

>Census 2000 · Estimates ·
>Projections · Housing · Income ·
>International · Poverty ·
>Genealogy

There are also categories for BUSINESS and GEOGRAPHY, where you can access maps. This is great place to go exploring. Some Census data is not based on the decennial population count, but on samples. Estimates based on samples require some "wiggle room," called confidence intervals.

Confidence Intervals

The Census Bureau estimates based on samples are accompanied by *confidence intervals*. What is a confidence interval? This data is based on *sample of*, not a full count of the *population of* McDowell County. Other samples taken from the same population would yield slightly different results. The confidence interval provides the range of possible scores for the other samples, indicating that in 90% of other samples, or nine out of ten of them, the sample scores will fall within the minimum and maximum values given. In the case of McDowell County in confidence interval for related children between 5 and 17 in poverty ranged from a minimum of 41.9 percent to a maximum of 72.6 percent. Note the wide range of the confidence interval, some 30 percentage points. McDowell's small population (29,916) requires a wide confidence interval.

Try a county with a large population, such as Kanawha, where West Virginia's capital, Charleston, is located, Kanawha's estimated 1998 population was 202,011, almost seven times as large as McDowell's. Kanawha County's 90 percent confidence interval for related children between 5 and 17 in poverty ranges from 17.0 percent to 26.5 percent, a range of less than 10 percent. Larger populations enable smaller confidence intervals.

Check out McDowell County, in the coal fields of West Virginia. *Click on* Select a State on the right-hand side of your screen. Choose West Virginia from the list. *Click on* Get State Profile. *Select* "McDowell" from the list of counties.

	McDowell	W.Va.
What was McDowell's population for the 2000 Census?	_____	_____
What was the median household income (199(7) estimate)?	_____	_____
What was the percentage of people in poverty?	_____	_____
What percentage of children were in poverty?	_____	_____

Let's leave the coalfields and check out Madison County, a rural county outside Asheville in North Carolina.

	Madison	N.C.
What was Madison's population for the 2000 Census?	_____	_____
What was the median household income (199(7) estimate)?	_____	_____
What was the percentage of people in poverty?	_____	_____
What percentage of children were in poverty?	_____	_____

Look at an urbanizing Appalachian County outside of Atlanta: Gwinnett, Georgia.

	Gwinnett	Georgia
What was McDowell's population for the 2000 Census?	_____	_____
What was the median household income (199(7) estimate)?	_____	_____
What was the percentage of people in poverty?	_____	_____
What percentage of children were in poverty?	_____	_____

The Census Bureau URL is only the tip of the iceberg for Federal agency data. Try www.fedstats.gov. More than 70 Federal agencies produce statistics. The Federal Interagency Council on Statistical Policy maintains this site to provide access to statistics and information produced by these agencies for public use. *Click on* "Agencies Listed Alphabetically." Under "E," *select* the Environmental Protection Agency. *Click on* air pollution. Choose the "maps" option and then click again on "Non-Attainment areas" and on "ozone" to see a U.S. map of areas having unacceptable levels of ozone. List the Appalachian *states* having unacceptable levels:

1) _____   4) _____

2) _____   5) _____

3) _____

Go back to the Fedstats Statistical Agencies page and *select* the Mine Safety and Health Administration. Use the agency's search window (in the upper left hand corner at this writing) and *type in* "20th Century." Select the hompage for "A Pictorial Walk Through the 20th Century." It begins with a Glossary of Terms, describing a

    colliery _____

    headframe. _____

    tipple _____

    trip _____

Good terms to know! Describe the Picture No. 9 on the walk: _____

_____

_____

Use the button at the bottom of the page to return to the MSHA homepage. Click on the "Fatality Information" button on the left side of the page. Count the "Fatalgrams" reporting deaths for the current year. *Calculate the percentage* of deaths that occurred in Appalachian mines.

    Number of fatal accidents _____.   Percent Appalachian _____

What about 1998?

    Number of fatal accidents _____.   Percent Appalachian _____

What about 1997

    Number of fatal accidents _____.   Percent Appalachian _____

What have you learned about mine safety in American and Appalachia?

_____

_____

_____

I work with a number of health-related agencies and community organizations. They often need county-level data for planning and grant writing. As is the case with most states, North Carolina has a State Center for Health Statistics. The center's URL is http://www.schs.state.nc.us/SCHS/. Go there and *select* Health Statistics. *Select* North Carolina Pocket Guide. *Select* the North Carolina Health Atlas and click on the link to the County Data Book. Choose "Mortality." You should be provided with a spreadsheet of county-level data. See if you can find the death *rate* from heart disease for Buncombe County. Is the county rate higher or lower than the state rate? By what percentage is it higher or lower? (See Chapter V. as to remember how to compute the percentage difference.)

  Buncombe County _____   North Carolina rate _____

  The Buncombe County rate is _____% above/below the state rate>

You now see that data gathering is also done at the state level. The U.S. Census Bureau provides a link to state data centers at http://www.census.gov/ftp/pub/sdc/www/

List the data sources in the state that interests you the most, together with their URLs:

    _____

    _____

    _____

As you have seen with your search engines, there are a number of sites dealing with Appalachian culture, history and resources. Here are some URLs to give you a start in Appalachia:

The Center for Appalachian Studies at Appalachian State University has a good site for links to other regional resources: http://www1.appstate.edu/dept/appstudies/

The Appalachian Studies Association, formed in 1977, is a nonprofit, multidisciplinary organization for scholars, teachers, regional activists and others whose work centers on the Appalachian region. The Appalachian Studies Association's mission is to encourage study, advance scholarship, disseminate information, and enhance communication between Appalachian peoples, their communities, governmental organizations, and educational institutions. Check it out at http://www.appalachianstudies.org/

The Appalachian College Association (ACA) represents 33 member institutions in the states of Kentucky, North Carolina, Tennessee, Virginia and West Virginia. Its URL is http://www.acaweb.org/

The Appalachian Center at the University of Kentucky, Lexington is a multi-disciplinary institute created in 1977 to link University of Kentucky resources with Appalachian communities in programs of Research, Instruction, and Service. This center's URL is http://www.uky.edu/RGS/AppalCenter/

Lees McRae College provides resources at http://www.lmc.edu/appstudies/links.htm

Appalshop is a media arts and cultural center located in Whitesburg, Kentucky, in the heart of the Central Appalachian Coalfields. Appalshop produces and presents work that celebrates the culture and voices the concerns of people living in the Appalachian Mountains. Appalshop began in 1969 as a War on Poverty program to train mountain young people in media production skills. Rather than leave the region to find work in the nation's urban centers, the young people created their own nonprofit media company and began making films about the culture and social issues of Appalachia. While devoted to a particular place, Appalshop's work addresses universal concerns. See http://ns.appalshop.org/

The Highlander Center in New Market, TN has been training grassroots leaders for nearly 70 years. Its URL is http://www.hrec.org. The Highlander library catalog is online. To get to it, go to the Highlander Home Page, and choose <HIGHLANDER>. This will allow access to the entire library catalog, including books, audio/visual materials and archives. The Highlander web page has links to other Internet sites of interest to community activists and researchers. Among them will be links to the catalogs at Wisconsin State Historical Archives and Tennessee State Library and Archives, both of which house Highlander archives, information on researching corporations, federal government information, environmental, labor and human rights activism, and African American issues.

The Mountain Association for Community Economic Development, located in Berea, Kentucky, has provided technical assistance to grassroots organizations in Kentucky and Central Appalachia since 1976. It has a business development program for projects with the potential of providing jobs to low income people, a Democracy Resource Center and an Entrepreneurship Initiative. Since 1994, MACED has sharpened its focus on sustainable development through the Sustainable Communities Initiative and the Central Appalachian Sustainable Forestry Program. MACED's URL is http://www.maced.org/

Women's Initiative Networking Groups (WINGS) is also located in Berea and is associated with MACED. It is a nonprofit organization that provides entrepreneurial training, marketing consultation and networking opportunities to low-and moderate-women interested in starting their own business. http://www.wingsnet.org/

The Brushy Fork Institute at Berea provides training and support services to mountain communities. The institute's URL is http://www.berea.edu/BrushyFork/default.HTML

Alan J. Banks, a sociologist at East Kentucky University, has constructed an excellent web page, with links to a variety of data sources, from local, state and federal agencies to think tanks and advocacy groups. His URL is http://www.socialscience.eku.edu/Ant/BANKS/classpage.htm

Before he retired from the University of North Carolina at Chapel Hill, David E. Whisnant developed a web page for his course "Hillbilly Highways: Appalachia and America." The web page includes examples of student projects (becoming experts on a mountain county through web page construction), historical maps and links to related topics. The URL is http://www.unc.edu/~whisnant/appal/Sylfal97.htm

Scott M. Pearson at Mars Hill College provides examples of biological research in Appalachian habitats and the use of GIS mapping in research at http://www.mhc.edu/users/spearson/home.htm. Mars Hill's Center for Assessment and Research Alliances (CARA) with community groups and agencies can be found at http://www.mhc.edu/cara/.

Within the mountains are regional web sites, such as the Mountain Area Information Center (MAIN) in Western North Carolina. Through its URL, http://www.main.nc.us, MAIN provides information on and links to resources throughout its service area.

Beyond the region, the "American Studies Web" at Georgetown University provides links on a wide range of subjects. The URL is http://www.georgetown.edu/crossroads/asw/.

What you have learned about quantitative methods and regional studies in this book should enable you to make good use of the data and other information available on the Internet. As the URLs above suggest, the Internet also enables you to network with groups and individuals sharing your interests and concerns. For those interested in Regional Studies, an Internet search can take you to programs across the United States and the world.

Good hunting, good luck and, most of all, enjoy your new skills and ability to discover!

Glossary

Appalachia
A mountain region in the Eastern United States, with widely varying definitions.

Appalachian Redevelopment Act of 1965
A law passed by the U. S. Congress, defining the Appalachian region as an area in need of development and which created the **Appalachian Regional Commission (ARC)** to plan and administer federal funds for regional development.

Analysis of Variance (ANOVA).
Bivariate technique for analyzing differences among group means. The independent variable must be categorical and the dependent variable interval/ratio.

Association
Relationship between two variables.

Bivariate Analysis
Analysis of the relationship between two variables.

Categorical Variable
A variable whose values cluster responses into a group or category, such as gender (male or female) or shoe size (10, 10½, 11, 11½).

Case
A unit of analysis for a study (in this manual, each county is a case).

Cell Frequency
Number in a table indicating count of scores with a given value or joint values.

Chi Square (x^2)
Statistic that compares the actual frequencies in a bivariate table with the frequencies expected if there is no relationship between the variables. Used for tests of statistical significance and for some measures of association in tabular analysis.

Codebook
Listing of information about variables in a data set.

Continuous Variable
A variable whose values can fall anywhere within a range, such as a percentage (0-100) or the length of your right foot

Correlation Coefficient (r)
Measure of association between two interval/ratio variables indicating the strength and direction of their relationship; summary measure of the extent to which cases are clustered about the regression line.

Correlation Matrix
An array of correlation coefficients.

Cumulative Percentage
Percentage of scores that have a given value or less.

Data
Records of observations on case variables.

Data File
Data set stored in a form that can be used by a computer.

Demographics
The study of human populations

Density
population per square mile

Dependent Variable
A characteristic of a unit of study that is affected by the categories or characteristics of another (independent) variable.

Ecological Data or Variables
Aggregate data or variables based on spatial or geographic units such as city districts, states, or countries.

Genuine Relationship
A causal association that does not appear to be explained by an antecedent variable.

Independent Variable
A variable presumed to have an impact on a dependent variable. Years of education (as an independent variable) may be associated with income level (the dependent variable).

Level of Significance
Probability that a relationship found in sample data occurs by chance if there is no relationship in the population.

Mean
Arithmetical average of all scores; the sum of cases divided by the number of cases.

Measure of Association
Statistic summarizing the strength (and sometimes the direction) of a relationship.

Metropolitan Statistical Area
Although the definitions and acronyms have changed from census to census, it is a city of at least 50,000 people and the surrounding counties with significant economic and commuting links to it.

Migration
People moving in or out of a area, usually measured in terms of ten year intervals.

Multivariate Analysis
Simultaneous analysis of data for three or more variables.

Negative Association
Relationship in which higher scores on one variable are associated with lower scores on the other variable.

Nominal Variable
Variable with values that are unordered categories.

Null Hypothesis
Assumption of no relationship in the population.

Ordinal Variable
Variable with values that can be rank-ordered but that are not measured with a fixed unit of measurement.

Outlier
Score on interval/ratio variable that is unusually low or high.

Parameter
Characteristic of a population. (See Statistic.)

Percentage
Standardized frequency assuming a total of 100 cases.

Population
Set of cases from which a sample is drawn and to which a researcher wants to generalize. (See Sample.)

Positive Association
Relationship in which higher scores on one variable are associated with higher scores on the other variable

r (Pearson Product-Moment Correlation Coefficient)
Measure of association for the relationship between two interval/ratio variables.

r^2 (Coefficient of Determination)
The proportion of variation in a dependent variable explained by an independent variable.

R^2 (Coefficient of Multiple Determination)
The proportion of variation in a dependent variable explained by two or more independent variables.

Regression Line (Least-Squares Line)
Summary line on a scatterplot that minimizes the sum of squares of residuals.

Research Hypothesis
A statement of an expectation about the relationship between variables.

Sample
Set of cases taken from a larger population of cases. (See population.)

Scatterplot
Graphic representation of relationships between interval/ratio variables.

Score
Case's value on a variable.

Spurious Relationship
A statistical association between variables that is not genuine but instead is due to other antecedent or intervening variables.

Standard Deviation
Measure of variation in scores; square root of the variance. (See Variance.)

Standardized Variable
Variable whose scores have all been converted to Z-scores.

Statistic
Characteristic of a sample. (See Parameter.)

Statistics
1. Numbers that summarize information. 2. Methods for quantitatively summarizing and generalizing information. 3. Characteristics of a sample.

Subset
Cases selected for an analysis on the basis of their scores on one or more specified variables.

Tabular Analysis
Analysis of the associations among variables by comparing percentage distributions.

Type I Error
Rejection of a null hypothesis that is true.

Type II Error
Failure to reject a null hypothesis that is false.

URL
Universal Resource Locator: the "address' of a web site

Univariate Analysis
Analysis of data concerning only one variable.

V (Cramer's V)
Chi square-based, symmetric measure of association for nominal variables.

Variable
Characteristic or property that differs in value from case to case.

X-Axis
Horizontal axis in a scatterplot, usually used for an independent variable.

Y-Axis
Vertical axis in a scatterplot, usually used for a dependent variable.

Codebook for the APCOUNTY File Variables

SHORT LABEL **LONG LABEL**

1) NAME NAME OF COUNTY

2) STATES MAP MAP CODED TO DIFFERENTIATE STATES

3) THREE REGN APPALACHIA BY NORTH, CENTRAL AND SOUTHERN REGIONS

4) APPAL CORE 179 COUNTIES CONSIDERED APPALACHIAN BY FORD (1962) AND THE FEDERAL GOVERNMENT.

5) HIGHLANDS FEDERALLY DESIGNATED HIGHLAND COUNTIES

6) CITY IN MSA, CMSA, PMSA, OR NECMA (1) OTHERWISE (0)

7) %URBAN90 1990: PERCENT URBAN
This variable is used by the following variable: 85) %URb90coll

8) %RURAL90 1990: PERCENT RURAL

9) %URBAN80 PERCENT OF POPULATION WHO ARE URBAN 1980 (CENSUS)

10) %RURAL80 PERCENT OF POPULATION WHO ARE RURAL 1980 (CENSUS)

11) %AMER.IN90 1990: PERCENT AMERICAN INDIAN, ESKIMO, OR ALEUT

12) %ENGLISH90 1990: PERCENT REPORTING ANY ENGLISH ANCESTRY

13) %GERMAN90 1990: PERCENT REPORTING ANY GERMAN ANCESTRY

14) %ITALIAN90 1990: PERCENT REPORTING ANY ITALIAN ANCESTRY

15) %SCT.IRH90 1990: PERCENT REPORTING ANY SCOTCH-IRISH ANCESTRY

16) %SCOTTSH90 1990: PERCENT REPORTING ANY SCOTTISH ANCESTRY

17) %IRISH90 1990: PERCENT REPORTING ANY IRISH ANCESTRY

18) %BLACK90 1990: PERCENT BLACK

19) %>64 90	1990: PERCENT OF POPULATION 65 YEARS OR OLDER
20) %<18 90	1990: PERCENT OF POPULATION 17 YEARS OR YOUNGER
21) POPULAT 90	1990: RESIDENT POPULATION
22) %MIGR80-89	PERCENT NET MIGRATION (CENSUS BUREAU: INCLUDES CALCULATIONS FOR UNDERCOUNTS)
23) SEX RAT.90	1990: NUMBER OF MALES PER 100 FEMALES
24) %WIDOWR90	1990: PERCENT OF MALES OVER 15 WHO ARE WIDOWED
25) SME COUN90	1990: PERCENT OF THOSE OVER 5 WHO LIVED IN DIFFERENT HOUSE IN SAME COUNTY IN 1985
26) NOT N HS90	1990: PERCENT OF THOSE 16 TO 19 WHO ARE NOT IN HIGH SCHOOL AND HAVE NOT GRADUATED
27) H.S.GRAD90	1990: PERCENT OF THOSE 25 AND OVER WHO HAVE A HIGH SCHOOL DEGREE (ONLY)
28) H.S.GRAD80	PERCENT OF PERSONS 25 YEARS OLD AND OVER COMPLETING HIGH SCHOOL ONLY 1980 (CENSUS)
29) MED.EDUC80	YEARS OF SCHOOL COMPLETED: MEDIAN SCHOOL YEARS COMPLETED BY PERSONS 25 YEARS OLD AND OVER 1980 (CENSUS)
30) COLLEGE 90	1990: PERCENT OF THOSE 25 OR OVER WHO HAVE COMPLETED SOME COLLEGE OR ASSOCIATE DEGREE
31) COLLEGE 80	PERCENT OF PERSONS 25 YEARS OLD AND OVER COMPLETING 1-3 YEARS OF COLLEGE 1980 (CENSUS)
32) PERCAP 92	PER CAPITA MONEY INCOME IN 1992
33) PCAP%US92	COUNTRY PER CAPITA IN AS PERCENT OF US PER CAPITA This variable is used by the following variable: 86)PC%US92COL
34) PERCAP 70	1970 PERCAPITA INCOME
35) PCAP%US70	1970 PER CAPITA INCOME AS PERCENT OF NATIONAL AVERAGE

36) DISTRESSED	APPALACHIAN REGIONAL COMMISSION 1988 DESIGNATION OF COUNTY ECONOMY. 1 SEVERELY DISTRESSED, 2 DISTRESSED, 3 MIDDLE, 4 STRONG, 5 VERY STRONG. This variable is used by the following variable: 87) DISTRSDCOL
37) UNEMP 91	1991: CIVILIAN LABOR FORCE UNEMPLOYMENT RATE
38) UNEMP 80	CIVILIAN LABOR FORCE UNEMPLOYMENT RATE (BLS) 1980 (BLS)
39) %POOR 89	1989: PERCENT BELOW POVERTY LEVEL
40) POOR>65 89	1989: PERCENT OF THOSE OVER 65 WHO ARE BELOW POVERTY LEVEL
41) POOR FAM89	1989: PERCENT OF FAMILIES BELOW POVERTY LEVEL
42) POOR FAM80	PERCENT OF FAMILIES IN POVERTY 1980 (CENSUS)
43) CHLD POR89	1989: PERCENT OF CHILDREN UNDER 18 BELOW POVERTY LEVEL
44) INFANT90-2	INFANT MORTALITY: 3-YEAR RATE - 1990-92 (ARC)
45) DR.RATE90	1990: ACTIVE NONFEDERAL PHYSICIANS PER 100,000 POPULATION (AMA *SUBJECT TO COPYRIGHT*)
46) %MALE/CH90	1990: PERCENT OF HOUSEHOLDS THAT ARE MALE HEADED WITH OWN CHILDREN, NO SPOUSE PRESENT
47) F HEAD/C90	1990: PERCENT OF HOUSEHOLDS THAT ARE FEMALE HEADED WITH OWN CHILDREN, NO SPOUSE PRESENT
48) AGRICUL%90	1990: PERCENT OF EARNINGS FROM AGRICULTURAL SERVICES, FORESTRY, FISHERIES AND OTHER (BEA)
49) %AGRI.EM90	1990: PERCENT EMPLOYED IN AGRICULTURE, FORESTRY, AND FISHERIES
50) MINING %90	1990: PERCENT OF EARNINGS FROM MINING (BEA)
51) %MINE EM90	1990: PERCENT EMPLOYED IN MINING
52) MANUFCT%90	1990: PERCENT OF EARNINGS FROM MANUFACTURING (BEA)

53) MANUF.$90		1990: AVERAGE PAY IN MANUFACTURING
54) %MANUF.E90		1990: PERCENT EMPLOYED IN MANUFACTURING
55) RETAIL%90		1990: PERCENT OF EARNINGS IN RETAIL TRADE (BEA)
56) RETAIL $90		1990: AVERAGE PAY IN RETAIL TRADE
57) %TRADE E90		1990: PERCENT EMPLOYED IN WHOLESALE AND RETAIL TRADE
58) SERVCES%90		1990: PERCENT OF EARNINGS FROM SERVICES (BEA)
59) SERVCES$90		1990: AVERAGE PAY IN SERVICES
60) GOVERN.%90		1990: PERCENT OF EARNINGS FROM GOVERNMENT (BEA)
61) %HLTH EM90		1990: PERCENT EMPLOYED IN PROFESSIONAL AND RELATED SERVICES IN HEALTH
62) %FARMS 87		1987: FARMLAND AS PERCENT OF TOTAL LAND
63) %FARMS '82		FARMLAND AS A PERCENT OF TOTAL LAND 1982 (CENSUS)
64) FARM SZE87		1987: AVERAGE FARM SIZE
65) FARM SZE82		AVERAGE SIZE OF FARM 1982 (ACRES) (CENSUS)
66) FARM VAL87		1987: AVERAGE VALUE OF FARM LAND AND BUILDINGS PER FARM
67) FARM VAL82		AVERAGE VALUE OF FARM LAND AND BUILDINGS PER FARM 1982 (CENSUS)
68) FED$/CAP90		1990: DIRECT FEDERAL EXPENDITURES AND GRANTS PER CAPITA
69) DEM.VOTE80		1980: PERCENT VOTING DEMOCRATIC (CARTER) FOR PRESIDENT (ERC *SUBJECT TO COPYRIGHT*)
70) REP.VOTE80		1980: PERCENT VOTING REPUBLICAN (REAGAN) FOR PRESIDENT (ERC *SUBJECT TO COPYRIGHT*)
71) DEM.VOTE84		1984: PERCENT VOTING DEMOCRATIC (MONDALE) FOR PRESIDENT (ERC *SUBJECT TO COPYRIGHT*)

72) REP.VOTE84		1984: PERCENT VOTING REPUBLICAN (REAGAN) FOR PRESIDENT (ERC *SUBJECT TO COPYRIGHT*)
73) OTH.VOTE84		1984: PERCENT VOTING FOR A THIRD PARTY CANDIDATE FOR PRESIDENT (ERC *SUBJECT TO COPYRIGHT*)
74) DEM.VOTE88		1988: PERCENT VOTING DEMOCRATIC (DUKAKIS) FOR PRESIDENT (ERC *SUBJECT TO COPYRIGHT*)
75) REP.VOTE88		1988: PERCENT VOTING REPUBLICAN (BUSH) FOR PRESIDENT (ERC *SUBJECT TO COPYRIGHT*)
76) OTH.VOTE88		1988: PERCENT VOTING FOR THIRD PARTY CANDIDATE FOR PRESIDENT (ERC *SUBJECT TO COPYRIGHT*)
77) DEM.VOTE92		1992: PERCENT VOTING DEMOCRATIC (CLINTON) FOR PRESIDENT (ERC *SUBJECT TO COPYRIGHT*)
78) REP.VOTE92		1992: PERCENT VOTING REPUBLICAN (BUSH) FOR PRESIDENT (ERC *SUBJECT TO COPYRIGHT*)
79) PER.VOTE92		1992: PERCENT VOTING FOR PEROT FOR PRESIDENT (ERC *SUBJECT TO COPYRIGHT*)
80) PRES.VT80		1980: VOTE CAST FOR LEADING PARTY (1=DEMOCRATIC 2=REPUBLICAN) (ERC *SUBJECT TO COPYRIGHT*)
81) PRES.VT84		1984: VOTE CAST FOR LEADING PARTY (1=DEMOCRATIC 2=REPUBLICAN) (ERC *SUBJECT TO COPYRIGHT*)
82) PRES.VT88		1988: VOTE CAST FOR LEADING PARTY (1=DEMOCRATIC 2=REPUBLICAN) (ERC *SUBJECT TO COPYRIGHT*)
83) PRES.VT92		1992: VOTE CAST FOR LEADING PARTY (1=DEMOCRATIC 2=REPUBLICAN 3=PEROT) (ERC *SUBJECT TO COPYRIGHT*)
84) DENSITY 90		1990: POPULATION PER SQUARE MILE
85) %URB90COLL		PERCENT URBAN COLLAPSED INTO PERCENTAGE QUINTILES.
86) PC%US92COL		COUNTRY PER CAPITA IN AS PERCENT OF US PERCAPITA COLLAPSED INTO 4 GROUPS

87) DISTRSDCOL — APPALACHIAN REGIONAL COMMISSION 1988 DESIGNATION OF COUNTY ECONOMY. 1 SEVERELY DISTRESSED, 2 DISTRESSED, 3 MIDDLE WITH 4 STRONG AND 5 VERY STRONG COLLAPSED.

88) PER CAP$81 — PER CAPITA MONEY INCOME IN 1981 (CENSUS)

89) STATESCODE — REGION'S 13 STATES CODED

90) DISTRESS95 — APPALACHIAN REGIONAL COMMISSION-DESIGNATED ECONOMICALLY DISTRESSED COUNTIES IN 1995.

91) DISTRESS99 — ARC-DESIGNATED DISTRESSED COUNTIES 1999

92) PERCAP 95 — PER CAPITA INCOME 1995 (CENSUS)

93) PERCAP%US 95 — PER CAPITA INCOME AS A PERCENT OF THE U. S. PER CAPITA INCOME, 1995 (ARC)

94) MIGR90-97 — PERCENT NET MIGRATION

95) POP97 — POPULATION 1997 (ARC)

96) UNEMP 96 — PERCENT UNEMPLOYED, 1996

Readings and Media Resources

A selected bibliography of recently published books on Appalachia:

Couto, Richard A.
    1994   An American Challenge: A Report on the Economic Trends and Social Issues in Appalachia. Dubuque: Kendall/Hunt.

Eller, Ronald D
    1982   Miners, Millhands and Mountaineers: the Modernization of the Appalachian South 1880-1930. Knoxville: University Press of Tennessee.

Ergood, Bruce and Bruce E. Kuhre, editors
    1991   Appalachia: Social Context, Past Present and Future. Third Edition. Dubuque: Kendall/Hunt.

Fisher, Stephen L.
    1993   Fighting Back in Appalachia: Traditions of Resistance and Change. Philadelphia: Temple University Press.

Gaventa, John
    1980   Power and Powerlessness: Quiescence and Rebellion in an Appalachian Valley. Urbana: University of Illinois Press.

Higgs, Robert J. and Ambrose N. Manning
    1996   Voices from the Hills: Selected Readings of Southern Appalachia. Dubuque: Kendall/Hunt.

Higgs, Robert J., Ambrose N. Manning and Jim Wayne Miller
    1995   Appalachia Inside Out. Knoxville: University of Tennessee Press.

Hinsdale, Mary Ann, Helen M. Lewis and S. Maxine Waller
    1995   It Comes from the People: Community Development and Local Theology. Philadelphia: Temple University Press.

Philliber, William W. And Clyde B. McCoy, Editors
    1981   The Invisible Minority: Urban Appalachians. Lexington: The University Press of Kentucky.

Crandall A. Shifflett
    1991   Coal Towns: Life Work and Culture in Company Towns of Southern Appalachia, 1880-1960. Knoxville: University Press of Tennessee.

Turner, William H. And Edward J. Cabbell, editors
    1985   Blacks in Appalachia. Lexington: University Press of Kentucky.

Suggested Readings and Media Resources by Chapter

Chapter II: Exploring a Region through Quantitative Data
    Ergood and Kuhre, Section I. What is Appalachia? Especially 1. the Appalachian Research Collective's "Why Study Appalachia?," 3. Raitz and Ulack's "Regional Definitions" and 5. John Campbell's "The Southern Highlands and the Southern Highlander Defined."
    APPALSHOP film: Appalachian Genesis

Chapter III: Cultural Diversity in Appalachia
    Ergood and Kuhre: II. Historical Background: 9. John Campbell: "Pioneer Routes of Travel and Early Settlements."
    Turner and Cabbell, chapters 6, 10, 11 and 16
    Higgs and Manning, pp. 27-76: "The First Inhabitants," and "The Mythical Heritage."
    APPALSHOP film: Ourselves and That Promise

Chapter IV: Demographics: Urbanization and Migration
    Couto, An American Challenge: Chapters 5 and 7: Population, Work Force and Social Capital.
    Ergood and Kuhre, III. Demographic Characteristics. Note especially Stephen E. White, "America's Soweto: Population Redistribution in Appalachian Kentucky, 1940-1986."
    APPALSHOP film: The Long Journey Home.
    Additional film about Appalachian migrants to Cincinnati: The Newcomers

Chapter V: The Appalachian Economy I
    Couto, An American Challenge:
        Chapter 3: Appalachia in a National and International Economy
    Ergood & Kuhre: Section V. The Economy: Especially note 26. Salim Kublawi, "The Economy of Appalachia in the National Context" and 27: Helen Lewis Fatalism or the Coal Industry.
    Eller, Miners, Millhands and Mountaineers, Chapters 2-4
    Gaventa, Chapters 2 and 3
    APPALSHOP film strip: Clincho: Story of a Mining Town.
    APPALSHOP films: 1) Coalmining Women. 2) Frank Jackson, Coal Miner

Chapter VI: The Appalachian Economy II
    Couto, Chapters 4-6: Work and Income
    Eller, Miners, Millhands and Mountaineers, Chapters 6,7
    Gaventa, chapters 4 and 5
    APPALSHOP films: 1) Fast Food Women
                    2) The Buffalo Creek Flood: An act of Man
                    3) Mine War on Blackberry Creek

Chapter VII: Voting Patterns and Economic Conditions
    Gaventa, chapters 6, 8-10
    Ergood & Kuhre, Section VI. Polity, especially Branscome's "What the New Frontier and Great Society Brought."
    APPALSHOP film: The Big Lever: Party Politics in Leslie County, Kentucky.

Chapter VIII: Race and Region: Minorities in Appalachia
    Turner and Cabbell provide a rich selection of readings from nearly 20 authors
    APPALSHOP film: Mabel Parker Hardison Smith

Chapter IX.: Appalachia: A Land of Many Definiitons
    Ergood and Kuhre, I What is Appalachia: 3. Raitz and Ulack, "Regional Definitions."
    7. Bruce Ergood, "Toward a definition of Appalachia"
    APPALSHOP film: Hard Times in the Country: The Schools

ABOUT THE AUTHOR

THOMAS PLAUT is a widely published sociologist who served on the faculty of Mars Hill University from 1977 until 2005. He is a cultural diversity and cultural competency consultant. He previously was a reporter for the Baltimore Sun. Plaut currently serves as a Service Applicant Screener and ACA Navigator at Pisgah Legal Services in Asheville, North Carolina.

License Agreement

READ THIS LICENSE AGREEMENT CAREFULLY BEFORE OPENING THE DISKETTE PACKAGE. BY OPENING THIS PACKAGE YOU ACCEPT THE TERMS OF THIS AGREEMENT. *MicroCase*® Corporation, hereinafter called the Licensor, grants the purchaser of this software, hereinafter called the Licensee, the right to use and reproduce the following software: **American Government:** *An Introduction Using MicroCase* in accordance with the following terms and conditions.

Permitted Uses

- You may use this software only for educational purposes.
- You may use the software on any compatible computer, provided the software is used on only one computer and by one user at a time.
- You may make a backup copy of the diskette(s).

Prohibited Uses

- You may not use this software for any purposes other than educational purposes.
- You may not make copies of the documentation or program disk, except backup copies as described above.
- You may not distribute, rent, sub-license or lease the software or documentation.
- You may not alter, modify, or adapt the software or documentation, including, but not limited to, translating, decompiling, disassembling, or creating derivative works.
- You may not use the software on a network, file server, or virtual disk.

THIS AGREEMENT IS EFFECTIVE UNTIL TERMINATED. IT WILL TERMINATE IF LICENSEE FAILS TO COMPLY WITH ANY TERM OR CONDITION OF THIS AGREEMENT. LICENSEE MAY TERMINATE IT AT ANY OTHER TIME BY DESTROYING THE SOFTWARE TOGETHER WITH ALL COPIES. IF THIS AGREEMENT IS TERMINATED BY LICENSOR, LICENSEE AGREES EITHER TO DESTROY OR RETURN THE ORIGINAL AND ALL EXISTING COPIES OF THE SOFTWARE TO THE LICENSOR WITHIN FIVE (5) DAYS AFTER RECEIVING NOTICE OF TERMINATION FROM THE LICENSOR.

MicroCase Corporation retains all rights not expressly granted in this License Agreement. Nothing in the License Agreement constitutes a waiver of MicroCase Corporation's rights under the U.S. copyright laws or any other Federal or State Law.

Should you have any questions concerning this Agreement, you may contact MicroCase Corporation by writing to: MicroCase Corporation, 1301 120th Avenue N.E., Bellevue, WA 98005, ATTN: College Publishing Division.

www.ingramcontent.com/pod-product-compliance
Lightning Source LLC
Chambersburg PA
CBHW080403170426
43193CB00016B/2792